100 SERMON OUTLINES
from the
OLD TESTAMENT

100 SERMON OUTLINES
from the
OLD TESTAMENT

By

JOHN PHILLIPS

MOODY PRESS
CHICAGO

ISBN: 0-8024-7816-6

8 9 10 11 12 Printing/GB/Year 91 90 89 88 87 86

Printed in the United States of America

CONTENTS

Introduction

INTRODUCTION

What constitutes a good sermon outline? Doubtless the personality of the preacher and his own particular style weigh most in answering that question.

Many people have difficulty in creating good outlines. Certainly it is a time-consuming occupation. Perhaps that is why so many of us avidly copy down other people's outlines with which we are impressed. There can be no doubt that a clear, concise outline is one of the essentials of a well-developed message. Given a well-pointed outline, a sound exegesis of the passage, and a few telling illustrations, most preachers are on their way.

Here are 100 outlines. They aim to be sharp, not fuzzy. They seek to chart accurately the passage or theme being explored. Some are short and pithy, others are longer and more detailed, and some are capable of being expanded into a whole series of messages. These outlines will help the preacher keep his points well in hand as he delivers his message. They will also help his listeners retain the highlights of his message.

With each outline an introductory paragraph is included. These paragraphs are designed to set the stage for the outline, provide a suitable introduction to the message, or suggest an illustration for one of the points.

One further word. These outlines need not be restricted to preachers. Most of them will be found helpful by Bible students in exploring Bible passages and themes for themselves. They can also be used for home Bible classes and by Bible discussion groups. May the Lord Himself be pleased to bless them to the salvation of many and to the building up of countless more in the things of God.

1

CREATION AND PHILOSOPHY

Genesis 1

The opening chapter of the Bible stands diametrically opposed to various human philosophies. In regard to these popular human theories the believer takes his stand not on the shifting sand of human opinion but on the bedrock of the Bible.

1. **In Opposition to Atheism**
   "In the beginning God"

2. **In Opposition to Polytheism**
   "In the beginning God"

3. **In Opposition to Pantheism**
   "In the beginning God created the heaven and the earth."
   The separateness of God and matter.

4. **In Opposition to Materialism**
   "Let us make man in our image"
   Man is like God, possessed of a spiritual nature.

5. **In Opposition to Evolution**
   "After his kind"
   The expression occurs twelve times. It locks each "kind" into its own category.

6. **In Opposition to Naturalism**
   "In the beginning God created"
   Matter is not eternal, nor is man a machine.

7. **In Opposition to Nihilism**
   "And God created . . . and God said . . .and God blessed"
   Man is more than a machine, determined or capricious, operating in a meaningless closed system.

8. **In Opposition to Existentialism**
   "And God said" (ten times), "and God saw" (seven times), "the evening and the morning were" (six times). "And it was so" (1:30).
   There is a historical basis for faith. The Bible does deal with concrete facts.

2

THREE TREES

GENESIS 3:8; JOHN 1:48; LUKE 19:4

Often a progression of thought can be developed by bringing together a series of similar biblical objects or statements. This kind of sermon is sometimes called a "concordance sermon" because it usually derives from that source. Used sparingly, this kind of sermon has its place. Think, for instance, of David's *"search me,"* Peter's *"save me,"* and Samson's *"strengthen me."* Or link together the occasions when double names are used—for instance, Abraham, Abraham; Moses, Moses; Martha, Martha; Simon, Simon—to mention just a few.

1. THE TREE OF CONCEALMENT (Gen. 3:8)
   Adam: the man behind a tree

   a. His Fall: "I heard thy voice"
      (That voice had previously thrilled him.)
   b. His fear: "I was afraid"
   c. His folly: "I hid myself"

2. THE TREE OF COMPLACENCY (John 1:48)
   Nathanael: the man beneath a tree
   Jesus shook him. He revealed that He knew—

   a. Where Nathanael had been reclining (v. 50)
   b. What Nathanael had been reading (v. 51; compare Gen. 28:10-12)

3. THE TREE OF CONVENIENCE (Luke 19:4)
   Zacchaeus: the man up a tree

   a. Why he ascended the tree (v. 3).
   b. Why he descended the tree (v. 6).

3

THE FALL OF MAN

GENESIS 3:1-8

Satan's attack on our first parents began with an attack upon the Word of God. God's Word, brief as it was in those days, was Eve's sole defence against the insinuations and suggestions of that subtle foe who entered Eden filled with the genius of a cherub. To all his craft and cunning she need only have replied, "Thus saith the Lord!" and Satan's sophistries and blandishments would have been parried. In the last analysis the temptation hinged upon the matter of belief. Would Eve believe God or would she believe the serpent?

1. SATAN'S ATTACK
    a. The doubt (3:1-3)
    b. The denial (3:4)
    c. The delusion (3:5)

2. SATAN'S ATTAINMENT (3:6-8)
    a. Eve's deception
    b. Adam's disobedience

NOTE: Satan's attack upon the Word of God was three-pronged. He attacked the *authority* of God's Word: "Yea, hath *God* said?" He attacked the *accuracy* of the Word: "Hath God said, Ye shall not eat of *every* tree?" ("How do you know that that is exactly what God said?") He attacked the *acceptability* of the Word of God by getting Eve to see the supposed benefits of abandoning it ("good for food," etc.).

4

THE FIRST JUDGMENT

Genesis 3:9-24

The sentence of death was passed upon Adam and Eve as soon as they sinned. The execution of the sentence was in stages. Adam died spiritually the moment he disobeyed God. He did not die physically until he was 930 years of age.

1. Adam Was Summoned (3:9)

2. Adam Was Searched (3:10-13)

3. Adam Was Sentenced (3:14-19)

4. Adam Was Saved (3:20-24)

Note: God's grace devised a means, way back there in Eden, whereby His banished need not be expelled from Him. Adam and Eve were both saved from the eternal consequences of their sin. Adam trusted in the promise of a coming Saviour, the "seed of the woman." He was clothed in skins at the expense of an innocent victim—a clear foreview of Calvary. He confessed his faith by calling his wife's name "Eve" (mother of all *living*) in the face of the death sentence recently pronounced.

Adam's judgment foreshadows the coming judgment of all lost men at the great white throne. The first question in the Bible will ring out again: "Where art thou?" and the wicked dead will come hurrying from their graves. The second great question, "What is this that thou hast done?" will be the great condemning question.

THE FIRST FALSE RELIGION

GENESIS 4:5-24

"The way of Cain!" It is set forth in the Bible as the antithesis of God's way. It is that "way which seemeth right unto a man, but the end thereof are the ways of death" (Prov. 14:12). Cain invented the world's first false religion. At its heart are the basic principles that animate every false religious system ever spawned upon this planet. Although it produced an impressive culture, it simply paved the broad road that leads to eternal night.

It was—

1. FATHERED BY SATAN (4:5)

2. FOUNDED ON "WORKS" (4:3)

3. FURTHERED BY VIOLENCE (4:8)

4. FATAL FOR MANKIND (4:16-24)

NOTE: One of the world's great authorities on the religions of mankind has pointed out that all false religions emphasize human good works and merit as the basis for salvation. He came to this conclusion after studying the sacred books of the East, the Koran of Islam, the Tripitaka, the Zend-avesta, and so forth. The same false philosophy animates the false teachings of the various cults and apostate systems of Christendom. It is only in the Bible that the word rings out loud and clear: "Not of works, lest any man should boast."

6

MY BROTHER'S KEEPER

The first human being ever to be born on this planet grew up to be a murderer, a reviler of God, an apostate, and an active leader in the development of a secular, materialistic, carnal, and seemingly successful worldly culture.

1. SIN DECEIVES
   (Eve mistook Cain for Christ. "I have gotten a man," she exclaimed, "the LORD" [Gen. 4:1, *New American Standard Bible,* marg.]).

2. SIN DIVIDES
   (Man's first recorded sin separated man from God. His second recorded sin separated man from man.)

3. SIN DESTROYS
   (The first person to die on this earth was murdered by his own brother.)

4. SIN DEADENS
   ("Where is Abel?" said God. Cain sneered back, "I know not: Am I my brother's keeper?")

5. SIN DOOMS
   ("What hast thou done? the voice of thy brother's blood crieth unto me from the ground.")

6. SIN DAMNS
   Cain went out from the presence of God. There is not the slightest evidence that he ever repented. On the contrary, apostasy is bluntly labelled by the Holy Spirit as going "in the way of Cain" (Jude 11).

WALKING WITH GOD

GENESIS 4-6; 5:21-24; HEBREWS 11:5; JUDE 14-15

Enoch was the first man to be taken to heaven by way of rapture rather than by way of death. His story is of perennial interest on that account. He and the age in which he lived furnish us with a prototype for believers today, who, like him, live on the verge of rapture. His story is in four parts.

1. SURROUNDING GLOOM (Gen. 4-6)
   He lived—
   a. Socially, in an Age of Permissiveness
   b, Scientifically, in an Age of Progressiveness
   c. Spiritually, in an Age of Presumptuousness

2. SAVING GRACE (Gen. 5:21-22)

3. SIMPLE GOODNESS
   a. His testimony Godwards (Heb. 11:5)
   b. His testimony manwards (Jude 14-15)

4. SUDDEN GLORY (Gen. 5:24)

NOTE: In Genesis 5:24 we are told concerning Enoch that "he was not," but in Hebrews 11:5 an extra word is added— He "was not *found*." The clear implication is that Enoch was not only missed but that people actively went looking for him. What a picture that presents of the dreadful loss millions will experience on this planet within an hour of the rapture! Think of the young people, brought up in Christian homes, who will look in vain for missing parents and of unbelieving parents who will be faced with the mysterious absence of those in their families who belong to the Lord.

8

A CANDIDATE FOR RAPTURE

GENESIS 5:22-24; HEBREWS 11:5; JUDE 14-15

Enoch was the seventh from Adam in the line of Seth. Just as lawlessness had climaxed in Lamech, the seventh from Adam in the line of Cain, so godliness climaxed in Enoch. It is interesting to note that he was a contemporary of Adam for a little over three hundred years and that he lived alongside the other patriarchs listed in Genesis 5 all his life. He was raptured about seventy years before Noah was born.

1. HIS TRIUMPH (Gen. 5:22-24)

2. HIS TESTIMONY
   a. He pleased God (Heb. 11:5)
   b. He preached to men (Jude 14-15)

3. HIS TRANSLATION (Gen. 5:24; Heb. 11:5)

ILLUSTRATION: Picture a heap of mixed metals, some of them even buried in the ground. Picture a strong electromagnet passing over that heap. It might contain lead and tin, iron and zinc, copper and brass, silver and gold. The magnet pulls out just one kind. It pulls out just the iron. The silver, the gold, the lead, and all the rest are left behind. Why does the magnet pull only the iron? For the simple reason that only iron has *the same nature as the magnet.* No wonder Jesus said: "Ye must be born again." Only thus can we receive the kind of nature He has.

9

THE DAYS OF NOAH

GENESIS 4-6; MATTHEW 24:38-39

Noah lived in an age that was ripening fast for judgment. The Lord Jesus drew a direct parallel between the days in which Noah lived and the days that would immediately precede His return. This should invest the days of Noah with special interest for us today and should focus our attention with marked enthusiasm upon those chapters of Genesis which describe Noah's age.

The days of Noah were marked by—

1. SPIRITUAL DECLINE (Gen. 6:3) *rejected truth, Enoch, Methuselah, Noah* Heb 11:4-6 *Jude 14, 15*

2. SOCIAL DILEMMA (6:1, 11)
   a. A marked increase in population 6:1
   b. A marked increase in crime 6:11 *imagination.*

3. SHAMELESS DEPRAVITY (4:19; 6:5) *false religion, Murder, bigamy* *Giants* *Carnal sons of God* Job 1:6-2: 38:6,7 Matt 22:30 Jude 6,7 II Pet 2:4-9 Ps 82:1-6,7 Dan 2:43 Isa 13:18-20

4. SCIENTIFIC DEVELOPMENT (4:20-22) *Mistook materialism for God's blessing. I Tim 6:6* *cities - music - Machines*

5. STRONG DELUSION (6:8-19; Matt. 24:38-39) *All seems well, No matter what the preachers say.*

6. SOME DEVOTION (Gen. 6:8-9) *a few religious nuts left.* *Some with a form of godliness - denying judgment. Enoch - Jude 14,15 Methuselah*

7. SUDDEN DESTRUCTION (6:7; 7:11) *comes suddenly, but warnings of great length. II Peter 3:8 I Thess 5:*

NOTE: It was the godless descendants of Cain, not the godly descendants of Seth, who produced the arts, the sciences, and the culture of the antedeluvian world. Cain taught men to settle in cities, giving rise to an urban society. It was Jabal who taught people agricultural pursuits, Jubal who gave men the refinements of advancing civilization, Tubal-cain who brought in an industrial revolution, and Cainite women who leaped to prominence. The Sethites lived for the next world, not this one.

10

PREACHING IN VAIN

GENESIS 6:14-16, 22; 7:13; 2 PETER 2:5

Noah preached for one hundred twenty years. His only converts were his wife, his three sons, and his sons' wives—just seven people in all. His ark was, in itself, a monumental message to his generation. It was a visible monument to coming wrath, a voluble call to men and women to flee from the wrath to come. The preaching of Noah fell on deaf ears. No doubt some mocked, some vacillated, some wrote learned articles as to why there could never be a universal flood. Noah entered the ark "pure from the blood of all men."

1. HIS COMMISSION (Gen. 6:14-16)

2. HIS COURAGE (6:22)

3. HIS CONVERTS (7:13)

4. HIS CONSCIENCE (2 Peter 2:5)

ILLUSTRATION: Picture Noah preaching what might well have been his last sermon to the godless people about him. The ark is finished and stands with open door, gleaming in its final coat of pitch. Noah is preaching Methuselah's funeral sermon.

"You all knew Methuselah," he might have said. "His father was Enoch, a prophet of God. His name means 'when he dies it shall come.' And now he is dead and it is coming, it is surely coming, the long-delayed judgment of God. But salvation has been provided for you all. Who will come and seek refuge in the ark? All that is needed is one simple step of faith . . ."

11

NOAH THE PROPHET

Noah's three sons were the founding fathers of all the families, tribes, and nations that populate the globe today. The great table of the nations in Genesis 10 shows how the various families spread out into all the world. Two chapters before we have the record of Noah's prophetic utterance concerning the destinies of the peoples that would spring from his sons. He ignored *Ham* but fastened upon Ham's son, Canaan, whom he roundly cursed. In the process of time the Canaanites overran the promised land and became so vile that God demanded their extermination. *Japheth* was given world dominion. After many centuries, with the advent of Cyrus the Persian, world dominion indeed came to rest on the descendants of Japheth and has been there ever since. Of *Shem* came the Semitic peoples, the custodianship of "the name," and, ultimately, Christ Himself.

1. CANAAN:
   SERVITUDE FORETOLD (9:25)

2. SHEM:
   SALVATION FORETOLD (9:26)

3. JAPHETH:
   SOVEREIGNTY FORETOLD (9:27)

NOTE: Satan always tries to frustrate the divine purpose. Thus it was that the world's earliest empires were Hametic and Semitic not Japhetic. The Egyptian, Assyrian, and Babylonian empires all seemed to belie Noah's prophecy. But when the hour struck for the doom of Belshazzar it struck also for the fulfillment of Noah's words.

GOD'S WORK IN A HUMAN LIFE

GENESIS 11:26; 12-22

One quarter of the book of Genesis is given over to the story of Abraham. We trace his path from the paganism in which he was born and nurtured to the lofty peaks of the sublime faith that made him, indeed, "the Friend of God" (James 2:23). At times we see him living on the mountain peak, at times we see him in the valley. One day he is living in victory, another in fearful defeat. Yet we see God maturing him step by step until he becomes "the father of all them that believe" (Rom. 4:11).

1. HOW GOD DISCOVERED HIS MAN (Gen. 11:26)

2. HOW GOD DETACHED HIS MAN (Gen. 12:1)

3. HOW GOD DEVELOPED HIS MAN (Gen. 12-21)

4. HOW GOD DISPLAYED HIS MAN (Gen. 22)

ILLUSTRATION: A visitor to the Holy Land some years ago met a potter whose small workshop was located on the outskirts of Bethlehem, adjacent to a large field of clay. Going into the workshop the visitor observed that the potter had *detached* from the clay one piece, which he held in his hand. The potter then began to *develop* his clay, pounding it, wetting it, softening it, and then shaping it under the pressure of his hands on his wheel. Finally, after subjecting it to the heat of the ing it, and then shaping it under the pressure of his hands oven, he *displayed* it on a rough bench outside his shop—the finished work of his hands. Thus exactly God dealt with Abraham as, indeed, He deals with us all.

13

A BELIEVER'S FIRST STEPS

Genesis 12:1—13:4

Abraham was one of the greatest and godliest men who ever lived. Yet his first steps in the path of faith and obedience were stumbling enough! How typical he is of us all. He left Ur of the Chaldees only to hurry off down to Egypt as soon as things began to go wrong in the promised land. Down there in Egypt he lost his testimony and had to be roundly rebuked by the worldly Pharaoh. Back in the promised land he quickly pitched his tent and raised his altar to signify that he was once more a pilgrim and a stranger on the earth.

1. Abraham's Revelation (12:1-9)

2. Abraham's Retrogression (12:10-20)

3. Abraham's Restoration (13:1-4)

Note: In Abraham we have illustrated the law of the second chance. True, God gives us no more chances after death to undo the failures and follies of this life, but, blessed be His name, He gives us many chances before! Thus He brought Abraham back to Bethel just as He brought Israel back to Kadesh; He sent His word to Jonah "the second time" and came twice to the prophet with the words, "What doest thou here, Elijah?" What a blessing it is that God does not cast us aside with our first failure.

14

THE BACKSLIDER

Genesis 13:1-11

Were it not for a brief note in Peter's second epistle we would have great difficulty deciding whether or not the truth of the matter was in Lot at all. Peter assures us, however, that Lot was saved. He calls him "that righteous man" and tells us that he "vexed his righteous soul from day to day" because of the vileness of Sodom. Lot had no altar or, as we would say today, he had no quiet time whereby to judge matters in the light of Calvary. Hence his terrible decisions. He never asked if Sodom were a good place to raise children—just if it were a good place to raise cattle.

Lot was—

1. WEAK IN HIS DEVOTIONS (13:5)

2. WORLDLY IN HIS DESIRES (13:10)

3. WRONG IN HIS DECISIONS (13:11)

NOTE: Lot's fatal choice led to the loss of both his fortune and his family and almost to the loss of his faith. Such is the high cost of backsliding.

Life is made up of decisions. We make hundreds of them every day—some major, most of them minor. Each decision changes to a greater or lesser degree the direction of travel as we journey towards eternity, and each decision has a bearing on our future. For the most part decisions are determined by desires. Our desires are determined by our devotions—or lack of them. This is the point to be made in this message.

THE WORLDLY BELIEVER

GENESIS 13:11; 14:11-14; 19:14, 30-38

Lot had a secondhand faith. He was a true believer, accounted righteous by God, just as Abraham was, but he lived a worldly and carnal life. His life is a landmark on the highway of time, set up by God, to warn of the folly of trying to live for both worlds. The Lord Jesus draws our attention to the seriousness of the error. "Remember Lot's wife," He says (Luke 17:32).

1. LOT'S CHOICE (Gen. 13:11)

2. LOT'S CHAINS (14:11, 14)

3. LOT'S CHILDREN (19:14, 30-38)

NOTE: It seems incredible that Lot, having been once overtaken in the judgment of the world and having been rescued by Abraham when all seemed lost, should actually go back to Sodom. But so he did. Doubtless he was lured there by the prospect of promotion. When next we see him he is in the gate of Sodom—he is one of the city officials. His relationship with such a warrior-saint as Abraham assuredly impressed the king of Sodom and secured for Lot this position. But what a place for a saint!—helping to administer the vile laws that made the sins of Sodom socially acceptable.

THE DOOM OF SODOM

GENESIS 19:1-38

The sins of Sodom have been resurrected in our day. They have always been present on earth, lurking down the back alleys and producing their disgusting horrors in furtive ways. Now they strut brazen and unashamed and demand the endorsement of society at large. God has never failed to judge a nation that has acceded to such demands. Our generation needs to be warned that Sodom's sins will reap Sodom's doom.

1. THE MORAL PERVERSION OF SODOM (19:1-11)
   a. The prevalence of Sodom's sin (19:1-5)
   b. The persistence of Sodom's sin (19:6-9)
   c. The punishment of Sodom's sin (19:10-11)

2. THE MENTAL POLLUTION OF SODOM (19:12-38)
   a. It corroded Lot's faith (19:12-26)
   b. It corrupted Lot's family (19:27-38)

NOTE: Our culture whitewashes sin. We call a drunkard an alcoholic. A thief is a kleptomaniac. The person who commits adultery is said to have had an affair. The person who indulges in the vileness of sodomy is said to be gay. God's Word strips aside these euphemisms and bluntly labels these sins by their proper name. God's abhorrence of sexual perversion is amply illustrated in the Old Testament in that the Mosaic law demanded the death penalty for homosexual sins and in the fact that God destroyed with fire the city that gave its name to sodomy.

THE REWARD FOR TRUSTING GOD

GENESIS 15

Nobody trusts God in vain. Abraham had just surrendered his claims to the fertile valley of the Jordan. Better to resign his rights than to squabble with his brother! Now God steps in to reward Abraham for his unselfishness and spirituality of life.

1. THE BUILDING OF HIS FAMILY (15:1-6)

2. THE BASIS OF HIS FAITH (15:7-12)
   a. An apprehension of Calvary (15:7-11)
   b. An appropriation of Calvary (15:12)

3. THE BRIGHTNESS OF HIS FUTURE (15:13-21)
   a. His personal future (15:15)
   b. His people's future (15:13-21)
      (1) Captivity predicted (15:13-14)
      (2) Canaan promised (15:16-21)

NOTE: It was bad enough that there should be strife between brethren. But that this strife should be carried on in the presence of the ungodly is noted by the Spirit of God as adding to its offence. It was Abraham, the spiritual man, not Lot, the carnal man, who took the initiative in bringing to an end this deplorable condition. Paul admonished the Christians at Corinth that they should suffer themselves to be defrauded rather than go to court and publicly fight with another brother in the eyes of the world. It is a high and holy standard, but Abraham attained it and so should we.

THE PATRIARCHS AS PARENTS

GENESIS 17:19; 25:28; 27:41; 34:1-2

The Bible has a great deal to say about families and how they should be raised. There are not only many direct statements on the subject, there are also numerous examples both of families that turned out well and of families that turned out ill. Many of God's choice saints had unruly children. Eli, Samuel, Jacob, and David are conspicuous examples. On more than one occasion, for instance, the behavior of Jacob's sons was a public scandal. There is, indeed, a marked decline in patriarchal parental authority which well repays careful study.

1. ABRAHAM'S FAMILY:
   MARKED BY DISCIPLINE (17:19)

2. ISAAC'S FAMILY:
   MARKED BY DISCORD (25:28; 27:41)

3. JACOB'S FAMILY:
   MARKED BY DISSIPATION (34:1-2; 37:2; 38:13-18)

NOTE: The more we study the bad behavior of most of Jacob's sons the more we marvel at the grace of God which founded the nation of Israel upon such men. God's sovereign purposes could not be frustrated by human failure. There was, however, a judgment seat at which Jacob's sons were arraigned and publicly rewarded or rebuked (Gen. 49). God's grace and God's government are never mutually exclusive.

IDOLATRY

Genesis 31:30

A human being can stoop to no greater measure of folly than to worship idols. Jacob's father-in-law was an idolater. His own wife, Rachel, was tainted with the same brand of spiritual insanity. When Jacob fled from Laban, Rachel stole her father's household gods and, when Laban came looking for them, calmly sat on them in order to hide them from him! Within the whole of the Bible there is hardly a more eloquent exposure of the stupidity of idolatry.

1. The Fact of Idolatry
   (Laban openly admitted that the sticks and stones he was hunting for were his *gods!*)

2. The Folly of Idolatry
   (These "gods" could not prevent themselves from being stolen nor from being ignominiously sat on. Nor could they proclaim their presence to their devotee.)

3. The Force of Idolatry
   (Only shortly before this incident, the true and living God had spoken to Laban [Gen. 31:24]. Yet still he called the idols his gods.)

Note: The only adequate explanation for the grip idolatry gets upon a human heart is that it is demonic. That is, evil spirits lurk behind idols and fasten upon those who worship them. Indeed Psalm 106:36-38 says as much.

20

FROM RAGS TO RICHES

GENESIS 37:5-19; 39:8; 40:6-7; 41:1-5, 45; 42:21

Often we think of Joseph as a type of Christ. And so he was.
Touch his life anywhere and Christ can be seen shining
through. But what are the practical lessons to be learned from
Joseph's remarkable life? How did he react to his circum-
stances? How should we react to ours? How can we, too, become Christlike in our lives?

1. How He Faced His Advantages
   a. His growing convictions (37:5-11)
   b. His good conduct (37:13)
   c. His great courage (37:19)

2. How He Faced His Adversities
   a. When he was first attacked—he wept (42:21)
   b. When he was fiercely assailed—he refused (39:8)
   c. When he was falsely accused—he ministered to others
      (40:6-7)

3. How He Faced His Advancements
   a. Joseph and his bride (41:45)
   b. Joseph and his brethren (45:1-5)

NOTE: There is not the slightest hint in Joseph's life of any
desire for revenge for the wrong his brothers had done to him.
On the contrary, he not only freely and fully forgave them,
but he so worked that, of their own free will, they confessed
one to another their guilt. The very love of Christ constrained
him in all his contacts with those who had so evilly treated
him.

JACOB'S FAMOUS LAST WORDS

GENESIS 49

Jacob was a prophet in his old age. The spirit of prophetic inspiration lighted up his dying hours. He saw far down the ages. As, one by one, his sons presented themselves at his bedside, he looked at each man standing there and summed up his character and, at the same time, foretold the entire history of his race. Genesis 49 ranks as one of the great prophetic chapters of Scripture.

1. EVENTS RESULTING IN THE FIRST COMING OF CHRIST (49:1-15)
   a. The preparation of the nation (49:1-7)
      (1) Israel to be a disappointing people—Reuben (49:1-4)
      (2) Israel to be a dishonorable people—Simeon (49:5-6)
      (3) Israel to be a dispersed people—Levi (49:7)
   b. The presentation to the nation—Judah (49:8-12)
   c. The punishment of the nation (49:13-15)
      (1) The people exiled—Zebulun (49:13)
      (2) The people exploited—Issachar (49:14-15)

2. EVENTS RESULTING IN THE FUTURE COMING OF CHRIST (49:16-28)
   a. The period of tribulation (49:16-21)
      (1) The polluted remnant—Dan (49:16-18)
      (2) The persecuted remnant—Gad (49:19)
      (3) The protected remnant—Asher (49:20)
      (4) The preaching remnant—Naphtali (49:21)
   b. The period of triumph (49:22-29)
      (1) The virtuous ruler—Joseph (49:22-26)
      (2) The victorious remnant—Benjamin (49:27-29)

THE SOVEREIGNTY OF GOD IN A LIFE

EXODUS 2:1-22

Moses was Israel's Abraham Lincoln, a man raised up by God to strike the shackles from a nation of slaves. He is a man of such importance in the Bible that he is named upwards of seven hundred times. His birth, as is the birth of all national heroes, is of very great interest. He was born in a time of national crisis—when the first attempt was being made in history to exterminate the Hebrew people. He was protected by the sovereignty of God and actually raised to manhood in the very courts he was destined to humble to the dust.

1. THE PROTECTION OF MOSES (2:1-10)

2. THE PROVING OF MOSES (2:11-15)

3. THE PREPARATION OF MOSES (2:16-22)

NOTE: Moses is so important a person in the Bible that not only is he mentioned by name upwards of seven hundred times, but he is mentioned in every section of the Bible and to get rid of him we would need to tear our Bible to shreds— which is just what the destructive, so-called higher critics have tried to do.

At the burning bush Moses was given a glimpse of the future of the people of Israel. The bush burned with fire and was not consumed. In all its long history in the midst of hostile peoples, Israel has never been either exterminated or assimilated. As God was in that bush, so God has been in the midst of this people.

PHARAOH VERSUS GOD

Exodus 5, 7-8, 12, 14-15

Pharaoh harnessed the vast resources of Egypt in his fight with God—and he lost. He is set forth in Romans 9 as the great example of how God asserts His sovereignty in dealing with rebellious man. For those who set themselves to fight against God cannot win. They find themselves overtaken at last either by God's grace or by His wrath.

1. PHARAOH'S PRIDE (Exod. 5:1-9)
   a. Pride of race
   b. Pride of place
   c. Pride of face

2. PHARAOH'S PERSISTENCE
   a. He was deluded (7:22)
      (by the magicians)
   b. He was deliberate (8:25, 28; 10:11, 24)
      (Note his attempts to make deals with Moses.)
   c. He was deadened (7:13, 22, etc.)
      (God hardened his heart.)

3. PHARAOH'S PUNISHMENT
   a. A lost sovereignty (14:5)
   b. A lost son (12:29)
   c. A lost soul (15:9-10)

NOTE: Pharaoh hardened his own heart long before God hardened it for him. The hardening process is traced to Pharaoh up through the first five plagues. After the sixth, God hardened Pharaoh's heart for him. Space was given him for repentance after the seventh plague; thereafter, Pharaoh proving adamant, God hardened his heart until He met him in judgment at the Red Sea.

THE PASSOVER

Exodus 12

God's characteristic way of teaching Israel in the Old Testament was by means of pictures and models. One such type (as we call these illustrations now) was the Passover. Celebrated annually, this feast was intended to remind Israel of the past and to portray God's plan of salvation eventually to be enacted at Calvary.

1. THE NEED FOR REDEMPTION
   (Israel was in the house of bondage and under sentence of death.)

2. THE NATURE OF REDEMPTION
   (It was centered in the lamb.)
   a. How the lamb was selected
   b. How the lamb was slain
   c. How the lamb was sufficient

3. THE NEGLECT OF REDEMPTION
   (This meant death when the judgment angel passed through the land.)

NOTE: There is a progression in God's revelation of the truth concerning the Lamb. In connection with Cain and Abel it was a lamb for a man; at the Passover it was a lamb for a house; in connection with the evening and morning sacrifice it was a lamb for a nation; when Christ came it was a Lamb for the world. Note, in connection with the Passover, this additional progression—"A lamb, the lamb, your lamb." Note, too, that sometimes a house was too little for a lamb but that the lamb was never too little for the house.

THE BELIEVER'S FIRST STEPS

EXODUS 13:21-22

Israel's wilderness experiences are intended to illustrate for us the initial steps in the Christian life. God allows various things to happen to us so that He can teach us and train us and mature us in grace and in the knowledge of Himself.

1. HOW GOD GUIDED ISRAEL (13:21-22)
   a. The cloudy pillar afforded Israel guidance that was—
      (1) Conspicuous
      (2) Conscious
      (3) Continuous
   b. But that did not mean that there would be no— *13-15 Orders before explination*
      (1) Disturbances (14:8-9) *Trust-*
          (the sighting of Pharaoh's chariots)
      (2) Disappointments (15:23-24) *3 days exactly as God wanted*
          (Marah) *(24,25 How to make bitter sweet.)*
      (3) Difficulties (17:1-7) *a retest of 15:22*
          (no water)
      (4) Decisions (16:14-30) *Obedience-or blessing becomes wormy.*
          (rules about the manna)
      (5) Discomforts (16:1-2) *one month later, Egypts curse forgotten*
          (the wilderness)
      (6) Dangers (17:8-16) *flesh Essaus family-*
          (war with Amalek) *Numb. 14:40*
      (7) Delays (19:1-3)
          (Sinai)

2. HOW GOD GUARDED ISRAEL
   a. Potential separation (8:22)
   b. Positional separation (14:19-20)
   c. Practical separation (14:22-28)

3. HOW GOD GLADDENED ISRAEL (14:30—15:1) */ ties that follow*
   Salvation - Think on This, not the difficulties that follow

THE SONG OF MOSES

Exodus 15:1-18

There were no songs in Egypt, just sobs and sighs under the taskmaster's lash. But as soon as Israel is redeemed the songs begin. We read: "Thus the LORD saved Israel. . . . Then sang Moses and the children of Israel" (Exod. 14:30; 15:1). It is by no accident that our hymnbook is almost as dear to us as our Bible. If we except Lamech's boastful chant in Genesis 4 (sometimes called "the song of the sword"), this is the first song in Scripture. Appropriately, it is a hymn.

1. THE EXALTATION OF THE LORD (Exod. 15:1-6)

2. THE EXECUTION OF THE FOE (15:7-14)

3. THE EXPECTATION OF THE SAINTS (15:15-18)

NOTE: The Lord (Jehovah, the God of the covenant) is mentioned by name twelve times in this song. His praise (v. 1), His power (v. 6), and His person (v. 11) are all celebrated.

Five times the enemy asserted his sovereignty, opposition, and defiance of God (the repeated "I wills" and the "shalls" of verse 9). God's answer was to blow with His wind (v. 10).

As surely as God had brought Israel up out of Egypt, so surely He would bring her in (v. 17). God does not offer us half a salvation.

THE TEN COMMANDMENTS

Exodus 20:1-17

Israel's legal code is contained in six hundred thirteen laws. These laws embrace all phases of life, personal and national, moral and spiritual, domestic and international. They probe such minutiae as bird-nesting and women's apparel and such matters as the rights and restrictions of kings and who can and cannot be a priest. A knowledge of the Law of Moses is a useful introduction to the gospel of grace. It lays a good moral foundation for the gospel. Paul says that it is, indeed, our schoolmaster to bring us to Christ.

1. Duties Godward
   Key phrase: *the Lord thy God*
   a. Thoughts
      (1) No other gods (20:3)
      (2) No graven images (20:4-5)
   b. Words
      (3) No profanity (20:7)
   c. Deeds
      (4) The Sabbath (20:8-11)
      (5) Obedience to parents (20:12)

2. Duties Manward
   Key phrase: *thou shalt not*
   a. Deeds
      (6) Thou shalt not kill (20:13)
      (7) Thou shalt not commit adultery (20:14)
      (8) Thou shalt not steal (20:15)
   b. Words
      (9) Thou shalt not bear false witness (20:16)
   c. Thoughts
      (10) Thou shalt not covet (20:17)

THE TABERNACLE COURT

EXODUS 27:1-8, 16-18; 37:8

The tabernacle was an object lesson to Israel. In the light of the New Testament we can see how richly illustrative it was. The outer curtains of the court, for instance, depict the insurmountable barrier erected by God against man. Yet there was a gate, a wide, wide gate supported by four pillars, inviting the sinner to draw near.

1. MAN AS A CONDEMNED SINNER
   a. Conviction (27:16-18)
      The lofty, dazzling curtains held up by pillars of brass.
   b. Condemnation
      The brass of the pillars. Brass always symbolizes judgment.
   c. Consent
      The gate. Coming God's way.

2. MAN AS A CLEANSED SINNER
   a. A radical cleansing from sin (27:1-8)
      The brazen altar. The blood sacrifice.
   b. A recurrent cleansing from sin (37:8)
      The laver. Cleansing by water (symbolic of God's Word).

NOTE: Cleansing by blood secures our standing before God. It is perfect, as perfect, indeed, as the precious blood of Christ can make it. Cleansing by water deals with our state, which is often one of defilement. The Word of God is the instrument the Holy Spirit uses to deal with our daily defilement (Ps. 119:9).

THE HOLY PLACES OF THE TABERNACLE

EXODUS 40:21-27; HEBREWS 9:1-15

The outer court of the Tabernacle illustrates *man's natural state* before God as a *sinner*. The holy places illustrate *man's new standing* before God as a *saint*.

1. OUR NEW STANDING AS SONS OF GOD (Exod. 40:22-27)
   The holy place
   a. Light from God (the lampstand)
   b. Life through God (the bread)
   c. Love for God (the incense altar)

2. OUR NEW STANDING AS SAINTS OF GOD (Exod. 40:21; Heb. 9:1-5)
   The holy of holies
   a. We see Jehovah there
      The Shekina cloud
   b. We see justice there
      The cherubim
   c. We see Jesus there
      The ark
      (1) My physical needs met in Christ (the pot of manna)
      (2) My moral needs met in Christ (the unbroken Law)
      (3) My spiritual needs met (Aaron's rod that budded)

NOTE: The cherubim are associated with God's government at the gates of the Garden of Eden, with God's grace in the tabernacle, and with His glory in Revelation 4. It is significant that the high priest of Israel, on the Day of Atonement, sprinkled blood on the Mercy Seat, which formed the lid of the ark. The cherubim, fashioned of one piece with the Mercy Seat, gazed inward and downward—forever occupied with the shed blood there.

THE OLD TESTAMENT PRIEST

EXODUS 28:1-30; 29:4-7; LEVITICUS 9:22-24; 21:16—22:16

Israel had no priest in Egypt. Priesthood is introduced only after the people have been redeemed. The Aaronic priesthood primarily illustrates the priesthood of the Lord Jesus Christ and, in a lesser way, the priesthood of the New Testament believer today. Christ functions as a Priest for His own people. The sinner does not need a priest, he needs a Saviour.

1. THE CALL OF AARON (Exod. 28:1-2)

2. THE CLEANSING OF AARON (Exod. 29:4)

3. THE CONSECRATION OF AARON (Exod. 29:7)

4. THE CLOTHING OF AARON (Exod. 28:2)
   a. The coat (Exod. 29:5)
      Expressive of the Lord's humanity
   b. The robe (Exod. 29:5)
      Expressive of the Lord's deity
   c. The ephod (Exod. 28:6-30)
      Expressive of the Lord's ability
   d. The mitre (Exod. 29:5-6)
      Expressive of the Lord's authority

5. THE COMMISSION OF AARON (Lev. 9:22-24)

6. THE COMMUNION OF AARON (Lev. 21:16—22:16)

7. THE CONDUCT OF AARON (Lev. 21:1-15)

NOTE: There were some features connected with Aaron which could not, of course, have been even illustrative of the Lord Jesus. The Lord Jesus never needed cleansing. We, as priests, of course do. The Aaronic priesthood only illustrates the Lord's *service* as a Priest. His *standing* as a Priest stems not from Aaron but from Melchizedek.

THE FIVE OFFERINGS

LEVITICUS 1-5

Failure to keep the moral law exposed the Israelite to punishment and death. The ceremonial law made provision for failure to keep the moral law. It is important to observe that the offerings did not *cancel* sin, they *covered* it until such time as the offering of Christ at Calvary could provide true cleansing.

1. THE GODWARD SIDE OF CALVARY
   Its preciousness (1-3)
   a. The burnt offering (1)
      The fulness of Christ's devotion
   b. The meal offering (2)
      The flawlessness of Christ's devotion
   c. The peace offering (3)
      The fruitfulness of Christ's devotion

2. THE MANWARD SIDE OF CALVARY
   Its purpose (4-5)
   a. The sin offering (4)
      The principle of sin covered
   b. The trespass offering (5)
      The practice of sin covered

NOTE: The first three offerings were called "sweet-savour" offerings because they pictured worship and devotion, both Christ's and ours. The other two were called "sin" offerings because they dealt with man's offence and guilt.

The trespass offering was invalid unless the sinner first sought reconciliation with the person he had wronged. He not only had to restore in full the value of what he had stolen, for instance, but he was required to add twenty percent to the price.

32

THE SEVEN FEASTS

Israel's seven annual feasts were actually a great, annual enactment of prophetic truth. The first four feasts took place within a period of fifty days at the beginning of the religious calendar. The symbolism of these feasts was fulfilled in the events relating to Calvary and Pentecost. Then came a break. In the seventh month the other three feasts were celebrated ("Atonement" was in fact a fast rather than a feast). These look forward to Christ's second coming. The truth connected with the first four feasts has been literally and historically fulfilled. The truth connected with the last three feasts will also be literally and historically fulfilled.

1. CHRIST'S FIRST ADVENT (23:5-22)
   a. Passover
      The death of Christ
   b. Unleavened Bread
      The church age
   c. Firstfruits (23:9-14)
      The resurrection of Christ
   d. Pentecost (23:15-22)
      The coming of the Holy Spirit

2. CHRIST'S FURTHER ADVENT
   a. Trumpets (23:23-25)
      The regathering of Israel
   b. Atonement (23:26-32)
      The repentance of Israel
   c. Tabernacles (23:33-44)
      The reign of Israel

NOTE: Two of the feasts are distinguished from the others in that they each run for a whole week. These two feasts symbolize a period rather than a specific event. Thus the Feast of Unleavened Bread anticipated the church age and the Feast of Tabernacles looks forward to the Millennium.

THE FATAL CHOICE

Deuteronomy 1:19-44

A wrong choice is usually serious. A wrong spiritual choice is disastrous. The Hebrews trusted God to bring them out of Egypt; they failed to trust God to bring them into Canaan. At Kadesh-barnea they made that fatal choice which condemned the nation to the forty years of wilderness wanderings and a whole generation to a second-class life and ultimate death. Many a believer has his personal Kadesh-barnea—the place where a decision is made that leaves its mark on the rest of life. Kadesh tells us it is possible to have a saved soul but a lost life.

1. How Israel Was Directed to Kadesh-barnea (1:30-31)
   a. The conditions of her salvation
   b. The continuance of her salvation

2. What Israel Discovered at Kadesh-barnea (1:23-25)
   a. The fruit (1:25)
   b. The foe (1:28a)   *Numb 13:32,33*
   c. The faith (1:28b)

3. What Israel Decided at Kadesh-barnea (1:26-27)
   a. Refusal (1:26)
   b. Rebellion (1:26)
   c. Retreat (1:43-44)

Note: Israel was without excuse at Kadesh-barnea. Think of all that the people should have learned of God. The plagues on Egypt, the Passover, the guiding pillars of God, the song of Moses, the experiences at Marah and Elim, the lesson of the riven rock and the outpoured water, the provision of the manna, the victory over Amalek, the Law, the tabernacle—all these were lessons intended to mature the people. They should have been ready for the giants. God always prepares us for the battles ahead.

THE FIVE BOOKS OF MOSES

Luke 24:27

The Lord Jesus loved the Pentateuch, the five books of Moses. He quoted from it each time Satan attacked Him in the wilderness. He endorsed its divine inspiration. He referred to Moses as its author.

Each of the five books of the Pentateuch has a different emphasis. It is an excellent idea, from time to time, to leave the pursuit of texts and topics and take the long view of Scripture. It helps put things into better perspective.

1. GENESIS:
   THE BOOK FOR SINNERS

2. EXODUS:
   THE BOOK FOR SONS

3. LEVITICUS:
   THE BOOK FOR SAINTS

4. NUMBERS:
   THE BOOK FOR SOJOURNERS

5. DEUTERONOMY:
   THE BOOK FOR STUDENTS

NOTE: There is a progression of truth in the five books of Moses. Genesis is the book of beginnings. It especially deals with the beginning of sin and its consequences as highlighted by its closing words—"a coffin in Egypt." Exodus is the book of redemption, the great need of ruined man. Leviticus deals with worship and communion, the proper exercise of the redeemed. Numbers sets before us the pilgrim experiences of a redeemed people. Deuteronomy, with its backward and forward looks, is filled with fitting instruction for those about to enter into the promised inheritance.

THE SIX CITIES OF REFUGE

NUMBERS 35; JOSHUA 20:1-9

If a man committed involuntary manslaughter in Israel he found himself in a dangerous position. The next of kin to the slain person was obliged to take up arms against him and put him to death. This person was known as "the revenger of blood." He had the full sanction of the Law behind him. But what of the man who had committed the crime? It was unpremeditated. It was an accident. The Law provided for him six cities of refuge scattered at convenient locations throughout the land. He could flee to one of those and there he would be safe from the avenger. The Law required that he remain in such a city until the death of the high priest, at which time the Law annulled his offence and he could go free. These cities, and their names, typify for us the salvation we have in Christ, and other blessings we have in Him besides.

1. BEZER:
   OUR SALVATION

2. KADESH:
   OUR SANCTUARY

3. SHECHEM:
   OUR STRENGTH

4. HEBRON:
   OUR FELLOWSHIP

5. RAMOTH:
   OUR ELEVATION

6. GOLAN:
   OUR JOY

THE SCARLET LINE

JOSHUA 2:1-21; 6:22; MATTHEW 1:5, 16

Rahab was a harlot. Probably she was a temple prostitute, a practitioner of the vile Canaanite religion, which raised immorality to an act of worship. Certainly she was marked for death by the Law of Moses once Israel's armies took Jericho. Yet God saved her! How and why He did so is a great lesson in grace and an excellent study of His so great salvation.

1. RAHAB'S DEGRADED CONDITION
   a. Her terrible past (Josh. 2:2)
   b. Her terrible position (2:15)

2. RAHAB'S DRAMATIC CONVERSION
   a. Fear (2:9)
   b. Fact (2:10-11)
   c. Faith (2:12-15)

3. RAHAB'S DARING CONFESSION
   a. Godward (2:18, 21)
      (the scarlet line)
   b. Manward (2:18; 6:22)
      (her testimony to her family)

4. RAHAB'S DURABLE CONSECRATION
   a. Her son, Boaz (Matt. 1:5)
   b. Her seed, Christ (Matt. 1:16)

NOTE: Rahab's faith is given an honored place in Hebrews 11. How like the grace of God to mention Rahab there, in that great Westminster Abbey of the faith! Think of the notable names not listed there—Elijah and Elisha, Isaiah, Jeremiah, and Daniel, for instance. The inclusion of Rahab's name adds lustre to the grace of God.

THE JUDGES

The period of the Judges lasted about four hundred thirty years. It was a period of national apostasy and moral pollution. Nevertheless, God had His remnant in Israel throughout the period, godly men like Boaz and his friends. And from time to time the darkness was lighted by the emergence of a judge, a man who would, to a greater or lesser degree, lead the people back to God.

The cycle of the times was one of *sin, servitude, sorrow, salvation.* The cycle went round and round. Each of the more prominent judges (except for Abimelech the bramble, who was a usurper) illustrates the kind of man God uses in times of crisis among His people.

1. THE EXPERIENCED MAN (1:12-15; 3:9-10)
   Othniel

2. THE EXASPERATED MAN (3:15-30)
   Ehud

3. THE EXHORTED MAN (4:4-24)
   Barak

4. THE EXERCISED MAN (6:11-40)
   Gideon

5. THE EXECRATED MAN (9:1-57)
   Abimelech

6. THE EXCOMMUNICATED MAN (11:1-40)
   Jephthah

7. THE EXCEPTIONAL MAN (13:1—16:31)
   Samson

MR. SUNSHINE

JUDGES 13:1-25; 14:5-6; 16:1-30

Samson's name means "shining like the sun." It gives us a clue to his life, which, like the sun, rose to great and splendid heights and yet set so quickly in a blood-red sky.

1. THE MORNING SUNRISE OF HIS LIFE (13:1-25)
   a. His godly parents
   b. His great powers
   c. His glowing personality

2. THE MERIDIAN SPLENDOR OF HIS LIFE
   a. His strict consecration (13:5)
   The Nazarite vow—
   (1) No wine
       appetite crucified
   (2) No dead body
       affections crucified
   (3) No razor
       appearances crucified
   b. His sterling courage (14:5-6)

3. THE EVENING SHADOWS OF HIS LIFE
   a. His abuse of grace (16:1-4)
   b. His abuse of gift (16:5-21)

4. THE GORY SUNSET OF HIS LIFE (16:23-30)

NOTE: A red sunset is a sign of a fine tomorrow. With the death of Samson the focus moves on to Samuel, who first began to curb Philistine power, and then on to David, who smashed it completely.

REDEMPTION OF A PAGAN

Ruth

The book of Ruth is an appendix to the book of Judges. It shows that God had a believing, godly remnant in the nation even in those dark days; that His redemption extended even to His banished; that He ever kept in mind His goal of bringing the Redeemer into the world.

Boaz, of course, pictures Christ, the Kinsman-Redeemer. Ruth is the alien, the outcast, brought through no merit of her own into an intimate relationship with the redeemer himself. The Law legislated against the Moabite so that the whole story illustrates sovereign grace and is a marvellous picture of God's plan of salvation for lost Gentiles.

1. How Ruth Was Sought
   a. The famine (1:1)
   b. The family (1:2-4)
   c. The funeral (1:3, 5)
   d. The fear (1:6-18)
   e. The field (1:19—2:18)

2. How Ruth Was Taught
   a. Her relationship to Boaz (2:19-23)
   b. Her rest in Boaz (3:1-18)

3. How Ruth Was Bought (4:1-22)

Note: It is interesting that Boaz is not mentioned at all in chapter 1. Ruth does not even know that he exists. But once he is introduced things move swiftly to their climax. In chapter 2 Ruth is in his field, in chapter 3 she is at his feet, and in chapter 4 she is in his family. Thus the Heavenly Boaz would draw the sinner to Himself.

BEWARE OF BACKSLIDING

RUTH 1:1-5

God's promises to Israel were all "yea and amen" in the land. Outside the land, the Israelite was either in a backslidden condition or else under the active judgment of God. Moab, particularly, was a sad choice of residence for an Israelite, for Moab was under divine interdict. Elimelech's name means "my God is King," but, his name notwithstanding, he denied the sovereignty of God in his life when he moved to Moab. He soon paid for it.

1. MOVING TO MOAB (1:1-2)

2. MARRIAGE IN MOAB (1:3-4)

3. MISERY IN MOAB (1:5)

NOTE: Ultimate responsibility for the disastrous family move to Moab comes to rest upon the shoulders of Elimelech, the father and head of the home. His name means "my God is King," but for all practical purposes Elimelech had denied the sovereignty of God in his life.

There is a basic difference between a backslider, which Elimelech was, and an apostate, which he was not. A backslider rationalizes his wrong moves and finds excuses for them—something Elimelech no doubt did, basing his move on the famine. An apostate repudiates, root and branch, the faith he once professed to hold. Peter was a backslider; Judas was an apostate.

A BACKSLIDER RESTORED

Ruth 1:6-13

The high cost of backsliding is seen clearly in Naomi's testimony and in her two names. The name "Naomi" means "pleasant"—that was her going-away name. "Marah" means "bitter"—that was her coming-home name. Her years in Moab had been anything but happy. There she had lost her husband, seen her sons marry pagans, and lost both her sons as well. Yet God blessed her and gave her back much more when she made up her mind to get back into fellowship with His people.

1. Naomi's Glad Tidings (1:6)

2. Naomi's Sad Testimony (1:7-13)
   a. The impact made by her walk (1:7)
   b. The impression made by her words (1:8-13)

Note: God leaves the apostate alone. Again and again in Romans 1 we read of certain ones that "God gave them up." He never gives up the backslider—He pursues after him. Thus Naomi heard the news that God had visited His people and a great longing sprang up in her heart to get back to the place of blessing.

Yet the backslider's condition is serious enough. Think of the terrible advice Naomi gave to those two girls down there in Moab— "I think you'd better stay down here. You'll have a much better chance of getting remarried." In Orpah's case the advice was all too successful. Often, in later years, Naomi must have been haunted by thoughts of Orpah hurrying on to a lost eternity thanks to the advice she had given.

QUALIFICATIONS FOR A STATESMAN

1 Samuel 16:15

David was whisked away from the sheepfold to the court. A country boy called upon to play the courtier! David needed no special training for that! He was a statesman born. It was second nature to him to play the part of a confidant of kings. The traits he displayed so well in King Saul's royal court should be marked and emulated by all who seek public office.

1. DAVID'S COMPETENCE
   (cunning in playing)

2. DAVID'S COURAGE
   (a mighty, valiant man)

3. DAVID'S CONQUESTS
   (a man of war)

4. DAVID'S CAUTION
   (prudent in matters)

5. DAVID'S CHARISMA
   (a comely person)

6. DAVID'S CHARACTER
   (the Lord was with him)

NOTE: David certainly fulfilled the promise he showed as a courtier. He became Israel's greatest king. Indeed, all subsequent kings ever to sit on the throne of David are measured by him. He becomes the divine yardstick by which all the others are castigated or praised.

43

ABIGAIL

1 SAMUEL 25; ROMANS 7:1-6

Abigail was married to a fool, Nabal by name, whose name means just exactly that—fool! She came between David and his avowed intention of dealing with her husband for his insults. Her husband died shortly thereafter, leaving her free to marry David. Her story illustrates in a most remarkable way our bondage under Law and our freedom in Christ.

1. HER NIGHTMARE BONDAGE
    a. Her husband was churlish in his character
    b. Her husband was childish in his concepts

2. HER NATURAL BEAUTY
    a. Her beauty of countenance
    b. Her beauty of character

3. HER NEW BRIDEGROOM
    a. How she met David
    b. How she missed David
    c. How she married David

NOTE: The Law does not have the capacity to make a person happy, for the simple reason that its demands can never be satisfied. It is "do this, do that, do the other" morning, noon, and night. It has no praise, nothing but criticism and condemnation for failure to live up to its exacting and relentless expectations.

How different it is when one meets Christ! The efforts to meet the demands of the Law become a burden and the soul longs after the love and life and liberty to be found in Jesus.

But the Law's bondage cannot be lightly set aside. The only way out is by means of death. Nabal's death paved the way for Abigail's marriage to David. The Law's claims die at Calvary, leaving us free to be "married to another, even to him who is raised from the dead," as Paul so expressively puts it in Romans 7:4.

44

ABNER: SAUL'S GENERAL

2 SAMUEL 2:4, 8; 3:1, 17-18, 27-39

He was King Saul's cousin, which may account for the high position he held in the land. He served Saul all the while Saul was king, which meant, of course, that he opposed David and implemented Saul's schemes against David. Upon Saul's death he tried his hand at king-making, setting up Ishbosheth as rival to David. Disillusioned at last, he went over to David's side and brought the rest of the nation with him. His story illustrates the gospel, with special emphasis on those who spend their lives fighting the claims of Christ but who, at last, give in.

1. HOW HE FOUGHT DAVID

2. WHY HE SOUGHT DAVID
   He became—
   a. Disenchanted with the results of the life he was living
   b. Disgusted at the rottenness of the king he was crowning (Ishbosheth)
   c. Disarmed by the royalty of the one he was opposing

3. WHAT HE BROUGHT DAVID
   He brought thousands over to him.

NOTE: Abner spent his life fighting David. But at last he surrendered to David's sovereignty and in the first flush of his new-found joy went back and preached one of the most remarkable little sermons in the Old Testament. "Ye sought for David in times past to be king over you," he said to the northern tribes; "now then do it!" He brought eight hundred thousand fighting men and their wives and children to David by his testimony—though he never lived to see it.

45

DAVID'S GENERAL

2 Samuel 3:21-30; 1 Kings 2:5-6

Joab was David's general. He was David's nephew, son of David's sister Zeruiah. He was a thoroughly competent man, ruthless, cold-blooded, fiercely loyal to David so long as it served his interests, and a first-class fighting man. He spent his life fighting in David's cause, but he never loved David, and in the end he was handed over by David for execution. His story contrasts with that of Abner. Joab illustrates those who profess to be on the Lord's side but who really do not belong to Him at all. Joab's story makes an excellent gospel message.

1. How He Behaved Himself
   He had—
   a. A family loyalty to David
      His mother was David's sister.
   b. A fundamental loyalty to David
      He subscribed to the facts that—
      (1) David was saviour
          Few could doubt that after the Goliath affair.
      (2) David was sovereign
      (3) David was sufficient
          With David, Israel needed no one else.

2. How He Betrayed Himself
   His true colors came to light in three great crises in David's Kingdom.
   a. The case of Abner
      Joab disdained the mind of David.
   b. The case of Absalom
      Joab distressed the heart of David.
   c. The case of Adonijah
      Joab disobeyed the will of David.

SOVEREIGN GRACE

2 SAMUEL 9

Here is another of those beautiful Old Testament pictures that so brightly mirror God's way of salvation for lost men. Mephibosheth was the grandson of King Saul, and Saul, of course, was David's bitterest foe. But God swept Saul aside and enthroned David in his stead. With the kingdom firmly in his grasp, David looked for some way to show "the kindness of God" to Saul's kin. He discovered Mephibosheth, sought him out, brought him to himself, lavished his gifts upon him, and sat him at his table as one of his sons. It is a thrilling story of saving grace.

1. How David Sought Mephibosheth (9:1-5)
   a. "Is there . . . any?"
   b. "Where is he?"

2. What David Showed Mephibosheth (9:3, 7)

3. Where David Sat Mephibosheth (9:7, 10, 11, 13)

NOTE: Mephibosheth suffered as the result of a fall. He was just five years old when the house of Saul crashed in ruins and his own father was slain in battle. He was brought up by his nurse, who did not know David. When Mephibosheth saw David's messengers coming he must have thought his death warrant was in their hands. Instead they brought a message of grace—"David would show you, Mephibosheth, the kindness of God. Come! Come, just as you are." And Mephibosheth came!

PAGANISM EXPOSED

1 Kings 17-18

Elijah's confrontation with the false prophets of Baal on the crest of Carmel is surely one of the most dramatic incidents in the Old Testament. What a setting! The high bluff of Carmel stretching away into the distance. The blue waters of the Mediterranean far, far below, stretching away off to the distant horizon. The massed multitudes. The king and his court. The hundreds upon hundreds of Baal's priests. The lonely prophet. The gauntlet thrown down to the cult to put truth to the test in a battle of miracles. And, finally, the exposure of the cult and the execution of the pagan priests in the drenching rain. It is a picture worthy of a preacher's best!

1. Proving Personally That God Lives (1 Kings 17)
   a. In the commonplace (17:3-7)
      (beside the drying brook)
   b. In the crisis (17:8-16)
      (beside the dwindling barrel)
   c. In the calamity (17:17-24)
      (beside the dying boy)

2. Proving Publicly That God Lives (1 Kings 18)
   a. Exposing error
      (mocking the prophets)
   b. Explaining truth
      (the altar, a type of Calvary)
   c. Expecting blessing
      (praying for rain)

48

WRONG PRIORITIES

1 KINGS 20:40

King Ahab had made a fatal mistake. He had befriended a man God had sentenced to death. It was all of a piece with the typical behavior of this godless king. The prophet came to denounce him in God's name—fearless men those prophets of old! He told the king a story, a veritable scorpion of a story with a sting in its tail just like the story Nathan had told to David. It is a story worth repeating, worth studying. It shows the folly of being busy with the wrong things—the special pitfall for preachers, pastors, and missionaries.

1. THE DEFINITE MANDATE

2. THE DELUDED MAN

3. THE DILUTED MINISTRY

4. THE DISPLEASED MASTER

ILLUSTRATION: In his book *The African Queen,* C. S. Forester describes the dilapidated old steamboat at some length. He describes the extraordinary exertions required of her skipper just to get up a sufficient head of steam to get her under way. The trouble was that there were so many leaks, so many faulty seams and joints, that the power was simply dissipated into thin air and only with the greatest difficulty could the old boat be persuaded to get up even so much as a fraction of her original power. Its power was diluted by erosion and neglect. The steam leaked away in all kinds of futile ways instead of being channeled to drive, with single-minded purpose, its engine down below. How like many an overbusy believer!

NAAMAN THE LEPER

2 Kings 5:1-14

In the Bible, leprosy is a universal picture of sin. It was looked upon as "the stroke of God," and on some occasions it certainly was, as both Miriam and Gehazi attest. Naaman's recovery from his leprosy illustrates how God cleanses from sin. First, he had to come to an end of his own preconceived notions, an end of his prejudices, and an end of his pride. Then he had to take God at His word and accept cleansing on God's terms.

1. His Miserable Condition (5:1)

2. His Mistaken Conceptions
   a. The wrong person (5:3, 6)
   b. The wrong price (5:5)
   c. The wrong procedure (5:11)
   d. The wrong place (5:12)

3. His Marvellous Conversion (5:14)

Note: Josephus thinks that Naaman was the man who, in a recent war between Syria and Egypt, had loosed off his bow at a venture and thus killed Ahab, bringing deliverance to Syria and victory to his countrymen. What a priceless treasure Naaman brought home from that war in the person of the little captive maid who not only knew God's power but had a full measure of His grace stored up in her little heart. What a wonderful little gospel preacher she was! Suppose she had harbored natural resentments against Naaman! Suppose she had cherished secret satisfaction in her heart that the man who had stolen her away as a captive should be a leper! Suppose she had said, "It serves him right." Then the world would have been robbed of this wonderful story of salvation. She is one of God's precious nobodies who have a great reward awaiting them in heaven.

THE WAGES OF SIN

2 Kings 5:20-25

The judgment of Gehazi is as full of interest and as weighty with import as is the salvation of Naaman. Gehazi was Elisha's servant and the heir to Naaman's leprosy. He illustrates what happens to those who abuse privilege and persist in sin.

1. Gehazi's Fatal Proposal (5:20)
   a. He saw salvation in the wrong light
   b. He saw sanctity in the wrong light
   c. He saw sin in the wrong light

2. Gehazi's False Pretences (5:21-23)
   a. His approach (5:21)
   b. His appeal (5:22-23)
      (1) How subtle it was (5:22)
      (2) How successful it was (5:23)

3. Gehazi's Foolish Persistence (5:24-25)
   a. How he concealed the treasure (5:24)
   b. How he concealed the truth (5:25)

4. Gehazi's Fearful Punishment (5:26-27)
   a. The startling revelation (5:26a)
   b. The stinging rebuke (5:26b)
   c. The stunning retribution (5:27)

Note: Gehazi allowed familiarity with holy things to breed contempt. As the servant of one of Israel's greatest prophets he heard and saw things denied to millions. Yet that very familiarity was his undoing.

THE IRON DID SWIM

2 KINGS 6:1-7

Elisha's miracles were much more mundane, on the whole, than those of Elijah. The incident recorded here is full of ordinary everyday interest. But the miracle is none the less spectacular on that account! And behind the miracle lurks a spiritual lesson. The lost axe head represents man's lost soul. The stick, cast into the Jordan, represents Christ, God's Branch, plunging into death and rising again, having secured the salvation of that soul. Looked at in this light, the whole incident blazes with the gospel.

1. THE SOLEMN CONDITION OF THE AXE HEAD
   a. Loss

   b. Liability
      ("Alas, master! for it was borrowed.")
   c. Limitation
      (The work came to a stop.)

2. THE SUDDEN CONVERSION OF THE AXE HEAD
   The prophet's "plan of salvation" was—
   a. Apparently very superficial
      (What good would it do to throw a stick into the river?)
   b. Actually very sublime
      (It prefigured Calvary—Christ's going into death for us.)
   c. Assuredly very successful
      (It worked!)

3. THE SILENT CONFESSION OF THE AXE HEAD
   a. What a task it now had
   b. What a testimony it now had

THE MEN OF ISSACHAR

1 Chronicles 12:32

Issachar was one of the lesser tribes of Israel. Its name does not ring in history nearly so loudly as the name of Judah or Benjamin, Ephraim or even Dan. Yet this tribe was destined to play an important role at a time of great national crisis in Israel. It stepped to the fore as a champion of David and a vocal advocate of his return. The part played by this insignificant tribe shows how God delights to use the "nobodies" of this world in order to accomplish His will.

The men of Issachar were men of—

1. Relative Insignificance

2. Remarkable Insight

3. Real Influence

Illustration: Little Bilney was a nobody. He was converted through reading the writings of Erasmus in the days when the Roman Church held sway in England. He felt his insignificance. He thought of Father Latimer, a popular and influential Roman prelate and set himself to win Latimer for Christ.

After considerable exercise of heart he went to the church where Latimer was preaching and, accosting the priest, asked permission to confess to him. Then he poured into Latimer's ears a confession the like of which the astonished priest had never heard before. Little Bilney confessed his emptiness of soul under the teachings of Rome and how he had found Christ and a peace that Rome could never give. He confessed his longing that Latimer, too, might find the same.

Thus little Bilney won to Christ a man who lit in England a flame that never went out.

A HIDDEN SAINT

1 Chronicles 4:9-10; 2:55

The first nine chapters of 1 Chronicles are made up mostly of names. What dull chapters they are! That is the instinctive reaction of most of us when first we find ourselves trying to plough down through them in a stubborn determination to read the Bible through from cover to cover. Yet here and there we come across a real oasis in this seeming wilderness. The thumbnail sketch of Jabez inserted here is just such a delightful stopping place along the way, illustrating for us the truth that no part of the Bible is really barren.

1. His Problem (4:9)

2. His Prayer (4:10)
   a. There was passion in it
      "Oh!"
   b. There was purpose in it
      "Enlarge!"
   c. There was perspective in it
      "Thine hand"
   d. There was persuasion in it
      "Keep me!"

3. His Promotion (2:55)

Note: The last verse of 1 Chronicles 2 tells us how God answered the prayer of Jabez. The scribes, the intelligentsia of the day, the leaders of society, the rulers of the nation, so honored Jabez that they built a city and named it Jabez and made it a city for the scribes.

THE GATES OF JERUSALEM

NEHEMIAH 3

Often, when reading the Bible, we can detect a second and hidden line of truth running beneath the surface of the primary and obvious meaning. We call this second strata of truth "typology." Nehemiah 3 is a case in point. The names of the gates point us to Christ, the One by whom alone we can gain access to God. The names of the gates not only speak of Christ, they depict aspects of the Christian life.

1. THE CALL TO SALVATION:
   the sheep gate (3:1-2)
2. THE CALL TO SERVICE:
   the fish gate (3:3-5)
3. THE CALL TO SOVEREIGNTY:
   the old gate (3:6-12)
4. THE CALL TO SUFFERING:
   the valley gate (3:13)
5. THE CALL TO SCORN:
   the dung gate (3:14)
6. THE CALL TO SUCCESS:
   the fountain gate (3:15-25)
7. THE CALL TO SPIRITUALITY.
   the water gate (3:26-27)
8. THE CALL TO STRIFE:
   the horse gate (3:28)
9. THE CALL TO SUNRISE:
   the east gate (3:29-31)
10. THE CALL TO SEARCHING:
    the gate Miphkad (3:31-32)

NOTE: The significance of some of these gates will be more apparent if the context is consulted. For example, the old gate was built by the rulers A good Bible dictionary would be helpful, especially in giving the significance of some of the names and symbols. The east gate is the gate of the sunrise—a thought connected with Christ's coming. "Miphkad" means "appointment" and reminds us that God has appointed the day in which He will judge the world. We are to be associated with Christ in that. Some identify the gate Miphkad with the prison gate.

A SUFFERING SAINT

Job 1-2

The book of Job gives us God's answer to the problem of pain. The book is in three parts. First we see Job in the hands of Satan, then in the hands of men, and finally in the hands of God. The greater part of the book is taken up with the dialog between Job and his three friends. Since none of them had all the factors in the equation none of them arrived at a proper solution to the problem posed by Job's sufferings.

1. How Job Faced Calamity (1:1—2:10)
   a. His blessings
   b. His bankruptcy
   c. His bereavement
   d. His boils
   e. His bitterness

2. How Job Faced Criticism (2:11—31:40)
   a. Anger (13:4-5; 16:2; 30:1)
   b. Agony (10:7-10; 16:11-17; 30:21-26)
   c. Assurance (28:29; 19:23-26)

3. How Job Faced Conviction (38:1—42:6)
   a. Rebuked by God
   b. Released by God
   c. Rewarded by God

Note: Job's friends were sorry comforters. They came to sympathize and stayed on to sermonize. All four of them, and even Job himself, are wrong in their arguments. None of them has the clue to the cause of Job's sufferings we have in chapters 1-2. None of them knew how it would end in Job's double blessing. All argue from insufficient data, a fault of which most of us are guilty when we criticize others.

LIKE A TREE

Psalm 1:1-3

Psalm 1 is anonymous. It is one of the "orphan psalms." Its
theme is God's Word and God's Word especially as that Word
is to be loved, pondered, and obeyed by His people. It shows
us God's Word as the great safeguard against the blandishments and philosophies of the unsaved man.

1. A Safeguarded Life (1:1)
   Protected from—
   a. The foolish advice of some
   b. The friendly association of sinners
   c. The full acceptance of scorners

2. A Spiritual Life (1:2)

3. A Successful Life (1:3)
   The happy man's—
   a. Prominence
      (like a tree)
   b. Permanence
      (planted)
   c. Position
      (by the rivers)
   d. Productivity
      (fruit)
   e. Propriety
      (in season)
   f. Perpetuity
      (leaf not wither)
   g. Prosperity
      (everything he doeth)

THE ATHEIST'S PSALM

PSALM 14:1-7

God calls the atheist a fool. In this psalm atheism is traced to its source in the human soul. The psalm reveals that atheism is not a mental problem but a moral problem. It is not that a person cannot believe in God but that he won't believe in God. He enjoys sin, indulges it, excuses it, prefers it above the knowledge of God. The very thought of God poses a threat; therefore God must be ruled out of the universe. Since the problem is not intellectual, the preacher should address himself to the conscience rather than to the reason when dealing with it.

1. THE FOOLISH MAN (14:1-2)
   a. The confession of human folly (14:1*a*)
   b. The cause of human folly (14:1*b*)
   c. The completeness of human folly (14:1*c*-2)

2. THE FILTHY MAN (14:3-4)
   a. Man's impurity (14:3)
   b. Man's impiety (14:4)

3. THE FEARFUL MAN (14:5-6)
   a. Suddenly confronted by God (14:5)
   b. Suddenly convicted by God (14:6)

4. THE FAITHFUL MAN (14:7)
   a. His longing
   b. His laughter

THREE FOOLS

Psalm 14:1; Proverbs 14:9; Luke 12:16-21

When God calls a man a fool we do well to pause and note that man. The Bible, especially the book of Proverbs, has a great deal to say about fools. (It is one of the ironies of Scripture that Solomon, the world's wisest man, had a fool for a son. No doubt many of Solomon's passionate outpourings on the subject of fools were inspired, humanly speaking, by Rehoboam.) Here are three Bible fools.

1. The Skeptical Fool (Psalm 14:1)

2. The Scoffing Fool (Prov. 14:9)

3. The Secular Fool (Luke 12:16-21)

Note: In connection with the skeptical fool it is worth noticing, both in Psalm 14 and in Psalm 53, that God traces atheism not to an intellectual root but to a moral root. It is not that a person *cannot* believe in God—there is plenty of evidence in the universe that God exists. It is that the atheist does not want to believe in God. And the reason is that he does not wish to face the consequent implication of responsibility for his moral wickedness.

The scoffing fool thinks sin is a joke and he jests about it and makes a mock of it. Sin is not funny. It is the great tragedy of the universe.

The secular fool does not have enough sense to know that money cannot buy welfare for the soul.

GOD OF CREATION

PSALM 19:1-14

Abraham Lincoln once said: "I can understand how a man could look at earth and be an atheist, but I cannot understand how a man could look at the heavens and say, 'I don't believe in God.'" Psalm 19 looks at the heavens. It shows that God has a double witness to Himself. There is His original witness in creation and His further witness in revelation. One is His witness in the Old Testament, the other His witness in what has been graphically called "the oldest testament." So then, we can find God either in the sacred Scriptures or in the starry skies.

1. GOD REVEALS HIMSELF IN THE STARS (19:1-6)
   The witness of the heavens is—
   a. Unmistakable (19:1)
   b. Untiring (19:2)
   c. Unlimited (19:3-4a)
      The stars—
      (1) Preach all languages (19:3)
      (2) Reach all lands (19:4a)
   d. Understandable (19:4b-6)

2. GOD REVEALS HIMSELF IN THE SCRIPTURES (19:7-14)
   a. His Word is precious (19:7-10)
      (1) How David described it (19:7-9)
      (2) How David desired it (19:10)
   b. His Word is powerful (19:11-14)
      (1) To convict (19:11)
      (2) To cleanse (19:12)
      (3) To correct (19:13-14)

AS FOR ME

The basic principles that governed David's life spring sharply into focus in a series of statements he makes in the psalms, each statement beginning with the expression, "As for me." "You can make your choice," he says in effect, "but as for me, here's where I stand." Thus he flings down the gauntlet to all who aspire to live life on the highest plane.

1. CONVERSION (Ps. 55:16)

2. CONDUCT (Ps. 26:11)

3. CONCERN (Ps. 35:13)

4. CONSECRATION (Ps. 5:7)

5. CONFIDENCE (Ps. 41:12)

6. CONTACT (Ps. 69:13)

7. CONSUMMATION (Ps. 17:15)

NOTE: Along the same line, link Psalm 18:30 ("As for God, his way is perfect") with Psalm 103:15 ("As for man, his days are as grass") and with Psalm 17:15 ("As for me, I will behold thy face in righteousness") and you have an excellent theme for a funeral service.

Perhaps David was stirred by the great example of that other great warrior of an earlier age—Joshua. In his last charge to Israel before his death, he reviewed the conquest of Canaan and threw down the gauntlet to the people he was about to leave. "Choose you this day," he said, "whom ye will serve; . . but as for me and my house, we will serve the LORD" (Josh. 24:15) .

THE LITTLE CITY

ECCLESIASTES 9:14-15

It was doubtless this little gem of a parable that inspired John
Bunyan to write his great classic *The Holy War*. In Bunyan's
book the city is the soul of man, beseiged and taken by the
evil one and enslaved to his will only to be retaken at last by
Prince Emmanuel. In Solomon's little story the city more
correctly, perhaps, refers to the world in which we live, its
ruin, and its redemption.

1. THE SIZE OF THE CITY
    a. It was small
        It had no outward significance
        (just like our planet in space)
    b. It was sparsely populated
        It had no inner strength
        (we are in a world greatly weakened by sin)

2. THE SEIGE OF THE CITY
    a. Its condition was helpless
        (there came a great king against it—Satan)
    b. Its condition was hopeless
        (he built bulwarks against it)

3. THE SAVIOUR OF THE CITY
    a. His presence
        (unknown)
    b. His poverty
    c. His power
        (his wisdom)

4. THE SIN OF THE CITY
    (no man remembered)

WHITER THAN SNOW

Isaiah 1:18-20

A skeptic once asked a Christian, "How does blood cleanse sin?" The Christian was nonplussed for a moment. Then he asked the skeptic a counterquestion. "How does water quench thirst?" The skeptic was now cornered. "I don't know," he said, "but I know that it does." "Just so," said the Christian. "You ask me, 'How does blood cleanse sin?' I say I don't know how but I know that it does." Sin! Scarlet, red like crimson! White as snow! Isaiah develops the theme.

1. A Remarkable Call (1:18*a*)
    a. Come! The appeal to the heart and will
    b. Reason! The appeal to the mind

2. A Radical Cleansing (1:18*b*)
    a. Like snow! A pristine whiteness
    b. Like wool! A processed whiteness

3. A Real Consequence (1:19-20)
    a. If! Joy set before us (1:19)
    b. But! Judgment set before us (1:20)

NOTE: The gospel invitation appeals to the whole man. Preaching should be directed to the *intellect,* for people must be able to discern how sane and sensible God's appeal is. There is nothing irrational or irresponsible about it. Preaching should be directed to the *emotions.* Joy and unhappiness, hope and fear, love and hate are powerful motivators. People must be stirred, made to desire what God offers. Preaching should be directed to the *will.* People must see that they have to decide, they must do something about it. Preeminently, preaching should be directed to the *conscience.* People must be brought under conviction of sin. That happens as the Holy Spirit brings passages such as Isaiah 1:18-20 to bear upon man's moral sense.

WOE!

How true the saying that history repeats itself. As we look upon contemporary society we can see the nations once more blossoming with all the sins that called for God's wrath upon Israel. Isaiah began his ministry by denouncing, in a series of devastating woes, the sins that were flourishing in apostate Israel. Were he to stalk the cities of our land today the same woes would pour from his lips.

1. THE SLUM LANDLORD (5:8-10)

2. THE GIDDY PLAYBOY (5:11-17)

3. THE SYNDICATE HOODLUM (5:18-19)

4. THE BEHAVIORAL PSYCHOLOGIST (5:20)

5. THE PINK PROFESSOR (5:21)

6. THE BESOTTED JUDGE (5:22-24)

7. THE AWAKENED SINNER (6:5)

NOTE: Like sins provoke like judgment. God is never in a hurry to pour out his wrath. In the days before the Flood he waited a thousand years from the birth of Methuselah until He caused the Deluge to come. With Israel and with Judah, He waited long centuries before He sent first the Assyrians and then the Babylonians as the ministers of His wrath. In the days of Abraham He postponed the fulfillment of His promise four hundred years because "the iniquity of the Amorites is not yet full," He said (Gen. 15:13-16). But when sin has finally come to a head in a nation, God acts in judgment according to fixed principles. That is why the world, apart from widespread repentance and revival, cannot escape divine judgment indefinitely.

64

THE MISSIONARY CALL

Isaiah 6

Chapters 1-5 record Isaiah's woes against the apostate nation of Israel. Now, standing in the spotlight himself, awed by God's presence, aware of God's burning holiness, Isaiah cries out "Woe is me!" His experience was similar to that of Moses at the burning bush and of Job after his great confrontation with God and of Daniel in the presence of God. God does not demand a golden vessel, but He does demand a clean one. Thus the first essential in the life of a prophet or a preacher is personal cleansing from sin. Three words sum up Isaiah's great missionary call.

1. Woe!
   The Prophet's Confession

2. Lo!
   The Prophet's Cleansing

3. Go!
   The Prophet's Commission

NOTE: Woe! That resulted from the prophet's vision of *deity*, he saw God. It was a vision of holiness. Lo! That resulted from the prophet's vision of *depravity*, he saw himself. It was a vision of helplessness. Go! That resulted from the prophet's vision of *duty*, he saw a lost world. It was a vision of hopelessness. These three interwoven elements are indispensable if a believer is to be used of God in his generation.

ISAIAH'S CALL

ISAIAH 6

Isaiah was a missionary—what we would call today a home missionary. His mission field was Israel and Judah. His task was to preach judgment, salvation, and revival. This famous passage records his call to mission work. It is of deathless interest because it embodies the basic elements that constitute any mission call.

1. THE VISION THAT ENTHRALLED HIM (6:1-4)

2. THE VISION THAT APPALLED HIM (6:5-7)
   a. How God convicted him
   b. How God cleansed him

3. THE VISION THAT RECALLED HIM (6:8-13)
   a. The call of heaven (6:8)
   b. The condition of earth (6:9-13)

ILLUSTRATION: Some years ago a missionary conference was being held at Moody Church in Chicago. In the large foyer of the church an interesting display was exhibited. It resembled a traffic light with red, amber, and green lights that came on and off at intervals. The amber light indicated the departure of a missionary for the foreign field. It came on once every thirty-five hours. The red light indicated the departure of a lost soul for eternity. It came on three times every two seconds. The green light indicated when every North American church would have given two cents to foreign missions. It came on once every twenty-four hours. The statistics may have changed, but the proportions are probably much the same. We should be ashamed.

BEWARE OF THE OCCULT

Isaiah 8:19-22

The supreme mark of apostasy in Israel was the growing popularity of the occult. All forms of occult practice flourished—spiritism, necromancy, witchcraft, astrology, soothsaying. The nation, having turned its back upon God, became an easy prey to demonic powers. It is remarkable what a revival there has been in occultism in our own day. A generation that prides itself upon its science is a generation that avidly hails the Satanist, the séance, and the soothsayer. Thus the prophet's exposure of Israel's folly is remarkably appropriate for today.

1. The Accursed Tryst (8:19)
    a. The proposal (8:19*a-b*)
        (1) "Try spiritism"
            (familiar spirits)
        (2) "Try Satanism"
            (wizards)
    b. The refusal (8:19*c-d*)
        (1) Positive
            ("Seek the God of your father")
        (2) Negative
            ("Shun the gods—i.e., demons—of your fathers")

2. The Accurate Test (8:20)
    a. The plumb line of truth
    b. The plainness of error

3. The Accounting Time (8:21-22)
    a. Endless problems (8:21*a*)
    b. Empty profanity (8:21*b*)
    c. Eternal punishment (8:22)

UNTO US A CHILD IS BORN

Isaiah 9:6

A child born! A son given! This one statement focusses both on Christ's humanity and His deity. One points us to the Babe of Bethlehem, the other to the Ancient of Days; one epitomizes impotence, the other, omnipotence; one reminds us that Jesus was Son of Man, the other that He was Son of God. But Isaiah's great statement does not restrict itself to the first coming of Christ. It leaps across the ages of His coming again. It takes us to the cradle, and then straight on to the throne.

1. THE COMING OF THE KING
   a. The mystery of the manger *Throne room*
      (1) The Child born
      (2) The Son given
   b. The majesty of the manger
      (the government on His shoulder)

2. THE CLAIMS OF THE KING
   a. Unerring in His decisions
      (Wonderful, Counsellor)
   b. Unquestionable in His deity
      (mighty God)
   c. Unending in His days
      (everlasting Father—i.e., "Father of eternity")
   d. Unrivalled in His domains
      (Prince of peace)

3. THE CROWNING OF THE KING
   (of His kingdom, no end)

COME THOU ALMIGHTY KING
Isaiah 10:28—11:16

The Assyrian invasion of Israel forms the historical background for Isaiah's prophetic judgments.

1. Israel's Aggressive Foes (10:28-34)
    a. The impending Assyrian invasion proved
        (1) The overwhelming miracle of divine prophecy (10:28-32)
        (2) The overpowering might of divine providence (10:33-34)
    b. The impending Assyrian invasion portended the future battle of Armageddon (10:28-34)
2. Israel's Almighty Friend (11:1-5)
    a. His acknowledged royalty (11:1)
    b. His accepted responsibility (11:2-3a)
        (1) Personal: as Israel's Messiah
            "The spirit of the Lord shall rest upon him"
        (2) Positional: as Israel's Monarch
            (a) All laws will be adopted by Him
                His *legislative* power
                "The spirit of knowledge and of the fear of the Lord"
            (b) All laws will be administered by Him
                His *executive* power
                "The spirit of counsel and might"
            (c) All laws will be adjudicated by Him
                His *judiciary* power
                "The spirit of wisdom and understanding"
    c. His active righteousness (11:3b-5)
        (1) The unique process of His government (11:3b)
        (2) The universal proof of His government (11:4)
        (3) The unifying principle of His government (11:5)
3. Israel's Astonishing Future (11:6-16)
    a. The redemption of a once-ruined planet (11:6-9)
        (1) All nature transformed (11:6-8)
        (2) All nations transformed (11:9)
    b. The restoration of a once-rebellious people (11:10-16)

69

THE REBIRTH OF THE STATE
OF ISRAEL

ISAIAH 11:10-16

No Old Testament prophet paints Israel's national future in more glowing colors than does Isaiah. The actual rebirth of the nation of Israel in our own day is one of the most significant signs of the times—an event of tremendous prophetic import. It heralds the approach of that era during which all God's great material promises to Israel, presently held in suspension by the intervening church age, will be fulfilled to the letter.

1. ISRAEL'S REDEMPTION (11:10)

2. ISRAEL'S REGATHERING (11:11-12)
   a. The examples of it (11:11)
   b. The extent of it (11:12)

3. ISRAEL'S REUNIFICATION (11:13)

4. ISRAEL'S REVENGE (11:14-15)

5. ISRAEL'S REFUGEES (11:16)

NOTE: The rebirth of the state of Israel is in defiance of the laws of history. When a people is uprooted from its homeland and scattered far and wide, history demonstrates that the dispersed individuals are assimilated into other nations. Immigrants, for instance, into the United States from Europe are absorbed within three generations. The original immigrants retain strong ties with the old country. Their language, their customs, their memories are all rooted back there. Their children are usually bilingual and have knowledge of the old country derived from the parents, but their educational and cultural ties are with the world into which they were born. The grandchildren often have few or no links with the old country. They are assimilated. The Jews have been scattered for *sixty* generations, and they have not only preserved their national identity but won back their ancestral land.

THE FALL OF LUCIFER

ISAIAH 14:12-17

Lucifer, of course, is the name by which Satan was known before his fall. He was once the highest of all created intelligences, standing as "the anointed cherub" (Ezek. 28:14) at the very apex of God's creation. Driven by ambition, he thought he could lead a successful coup against the throne of God. Great was his fall.

1. HIS POWER WAS ABORTED (14:12)
   a. His first rebellion—cast down from heaven (14:12a)
   b. His final rebellion—cast down to earth (14:12b)
      (1) The Battle of Megiddo (See Rev. 16:13-16)
      (2) The Battle of Magog (Rev. 20:7-10)

2. HIS PLANS WERE ABSURD (Isa. 14:13-14)
   He coveted that which belonged to God alone—
   a. God's raised position ("into heaven")
   b. God's ruling power ("the stars," i.e., the angels)
   c. God's royal palace ("the mount")
   d. God's regal presence ("the clouds")
   e. God's rightful preeminence ("like the most High")

3. HIS PRIDE WILL BE ABASED (14:15-17)
   a. He will be destroyed in hell (14:15)
   b. He will be derided in hell (14:16-17)
      (1) The mocking title ("the man") (14:16a)
      (2) The mocking taunts (14:16b-17)
         Where now is your power to—
         (a) Impress mankind (14:16b)
         (b) Imperil mankind (14:17a)
         (c) Imprison mankind (14:17b)

71

THE OLD TESTAMENT AND "TONGUES"

Isaiah 28:1-13; 1 Corinthians 14:21

Isaiah prophesied that tongues would be given as a sign to the nation of Israel. Paul refers to the prophecy in seeking to correct the abuse of the tongues gift at Corinth. In its proper context, this Old Testament prediction regarding tongues is most significant. The dreaded Assyrian invasion was at the doors. The prophecy about "tongues" was a judgment prophecy—tongues was a judgment sign, not a sign of blessing. Carry that thought over into 1 Corinthians 14 and the whole question of tongues takes on a different color from that which is generally presented. In particular, compare Isaiah 28:11 with 1 Corinthians 14:21.

1. Disaster Looming on the Horizon (28:1-6)
   a. The full extent of the disaster (28:1-4)
      (1) Pride to be abased (28:1-3)
      (2) Prosperity to be abolished (28:4)
   b. The future exception to the disaster (28:5-6)
      (the remnant)

2. Drunkards Leaning on the Helm (28:7-8)
   a. Their disgraceful behavior (28:7)
   b. Their disgusting banquets (28:8)

3. Darkness Leading by the Hand (28:9-13)
   a. The drunken folly of the Hebrews (28:9-10)
      (1) Intoxicated belligerence (28:9)
      (2) Intoxicated babblings (28:10)
   b. The dreadful future of the Hebrews (28:11-13)
      (1) Its character (28:11)
      (2) Its cause (28:12)
      (3) Its consequences (28:13)

NOTE: Examine verses 10 and 11 in context. The drunken babblings lead directly to the "tongues" that were to overtake the nation.

THE FORBIDDEN CHAPTER

ISAIAH 53

Isaiah's foreview of Calvary in this chapter is so remarkable, so clear and comprehensive, so undeniable that the Jews avoid the chapter like the plague. They cannot deny that it is part of Isaiah's prophecy. If pressed, they will interpret the Servant as Israel rather than as the Messiah although they are exegetically hard pressed to substantiate the evasion. So they avoid the chapter. In their liturgies in the synagogue they deliberately pass over Isaiah 53 as though it were not there.

1. APPROACHING CALVARY (53:1-3)

2. APPROPRIATING CALVARY (53:4-6)

3. APPREHENDING CALVARY (53:7-12)

ILLUSTRATION: We know, of course, that the chapter divisions of the Bible are not inspired. They have been added for convenience. Sometimes the choice of division is unfortunate. Still, there is an interesting phenomena discernible in the chapter divisions of Isaiah. In the first place there are sixty-six chapters, just as there are sixty-six books in the Bible. The major break comes at chapter 40, which divides the prophecy into thirty-nine chapters and twenty-seven chapters—corresponding to the number of books in the Old and New Testaments respectively. The first section of Isaiah has a distinctly Old Testament flavor to it, but the second section rings like a New Testament evangel. The twenty-seven chapters of Isaiah 40-66 divide into three sections, each of nine chapters, and the very center chapter is Isaiah 53. This almost seems more than accidental.

WOUNDED FOR ME

Isaiah 53:5

A surgeon, looking at this verse, instantly saw Calvary. He pointed out that there are five kinds of wounds that can be inflicted on the human body. Jesus bore them all. Truly, He was "wounded for our transgressions."

1. A Contusion
   The Lord suffered this kind of wound when He was hit on the head with the reed and when He was punched in the face.

2. A Laceration
   The scourge would produce this kind of wound. It was a vicious instrument like a cat-o-nine-tails, only its thongs were tipped with steel claws.

3. A Penetration
   The crown of thorns would produce these wounds. The Jerusalem thorn has great, long spikes. It was forced down upon His head and further pressed home by the blows of the reed.

4. A Perforation
   The nails, of course, perforated, piercing right through His hands and His feet.

5. An Incision
   The spear, cutting into His side, made an incision. The blood and water which flowed were, of course, medical evidence that Jesus was truly dead.

THE REJECTED CHRIST

ISAIAH 53:1-3

Isaiah's great prophecy of Calvary begins with the rejection of Christ by the Jewish people. This rejection of theirs mirrors the rejection of Christ by all sinners who, when confronted with the gospel, turn away from Him.

1. THE SCRIPTURES REJECTED (53:1)

2. THE SAVIOUR REJECTED (53:2-3)
   a. The unknown child (53:2a)
      (1) His promised appearing
         (a) His nature
             ("a tender plant")
         (b) His nurture
             ("a root out of a dry ground")
      (2) His personal appearance
          ("no form nor comeliness")
   b. The unwanted Christ (53:2b-3)
      (1) Revealed
      (2) Repudiated

ILLUSTRATION: A gardener points out that plants are divided into three categories—hardy, half-hardy, and tender. A hardy plant is one that is native to the area in which it is to be grown. A half-hardy plant is one that will readily adapt to the area. A tender plant is an exotic plant, one from another place altogether; it does not take kindly to its new environment, which it finds hostile to its nature.

THE SUFFERINGS OF CHRIST

Isaiah 53:4-6

D. L. Moody was once about to board a train when he was approached by a man who wished to know how to be saved. The train was about to leave and Moody had but one moment to spare. "Isaiah 53:6," said Mr. Moody as the conductor waved his flag, "Isaiah 53:6. Go in at the first 'all' and go out at the second one." The train moved away and the man went home. He looked up the verse, did as he was told, and was soundly saved.

1. The Reality of Christ's Sufferings (53:4)
   a. Bearing the burden of our sins
   b. Bearing the blame for our sins

2. The Reason for His Sufferings (53:5)
   Our sin is viewed as:
   a. An indebtedness that must be properly paid
      ("Wounded for our transgressions"—the idea is that of the trespass offering, where restitution was essential.)
   b. An iniquity that must be properly punished
      (He was "bruised," that is, "crushed," for our iniquities.)
   c. An injury that must be properly prescribed
      ("With his stripes we are healed"—as the hymn says: "None else could heal all our soul's diseases.")

3. The Result of His Sufferings (53:6)
   a. How God sees the problem
   b. How God solved the problem

THE LORD'S VIOLENT DEATH

ISAIAH 53:7-8

In the beloved King James Version, the wording of some of the prophecies can sometimes cause confusion and difficulty. Majestic as the cadences are in Isaiah 53, we need help in getting the message from the King James text. In verse 7 the word "oppressed" means "hard pressed." In verse 8, "taken from prison and from judgment" is better rendered, "by constraint and by sentence." "Who shall declare his generation" would seem to refer to the Lord's genealogy. Had this been honestly faced by the Jews it would have proven His claim to be the Messiah. "Cut off" is "wrenched," a graphic word for a violent death.

1. HIS SILENCE (53:7)
    a. Before the Hebrews (53:7a)
        ("Oppressed"—that is, "hard pressed"—and "afflicted")
    b. Before the heathen (53:7b)
        (1) Before Herod
            (as a sheep before the shearer)
        (2) Before Pilate
            (led as a lamb to the slaughter)

2. HIS SUFFERING (53:8)
    a. The invocation of the death sentence
        ("taken from prison and from judgment")
    b. The injustice of the death sentence
        ("who shall declare his generation?")
    c. The infliction of the death sentence
        (1) His was a vicious death
            ("cut off")
        (2) His was a vicarious death
            ("for the transgression of my people")

THE BURIAL OF JESUS

Isaiah 53:9

The Jews planned to cast the body of Jesus into the valley of Hinnom—what we would call today the garbage dump. The bodies of crucified criminals were normally disposed of in this way. In the valley of Hinnom the fires continually burned, making the place a natural type of hell itself. God planned otherwise. Once the soldier's spear had rent the Saviour's side, all human indignities ceased. From then on only loving hands touched Him and only loving hearts planned.

1. The Grave That Was Planned for Him by His Foes
   "with the wicked"

2. The Grave That Was Prepared for Him by His Friends
   a. The divine provision
      "with the rich"
   b. The divine proclamation
      "because"
      (1) Blameless in his walk
      (2) Blameless in his talk

Note: It is interesting that two Josephs figure in the human life of Jesus. God had a Joseph ready to play the father's part when He sent His Son into the world to be born of the virgin. He also had a Joseph ready to be His undertaker and take care of his entombment. Thus at His birth and at His burial a man named Joseph ministered to the Son of God.

THE RESURRECTION OF JESUS

Isaiah 53:10

Isaiah's foreview of the death of Christ reached beyond the grave to Christ's victory over the tomb. His language, ambiguous perhaps at times, comes wonderfully to life in the light of the actual event.

1. The Tragedy of the Cross Reviewed
   a. The unfathomable mystery of Calvary
      "it pleased the Lord to bruise him"
   b. The unforgettable ministry of Calvary
      "his soul an offering for sin"

2. The Triumph of the Cross Revealed
   a. Express proof of His holiness
   b. Executive power in His hands

Illustration: Lord Lyttleton and Gilbert West were both convinced that Christianity was a hoax. They agreed together that the entire fabrication could be torn to shreds simply by disproving the resurrection of Christ and by discrediting the conversion of Saul of Tarsus. Lord Lyttleton undertook to disrobe Paul and Gilbert West agreed to debunk the resurrection myth. When they met some time later to compare notes and progress each betrayed a reluctance to begin. Then each discovered that the other had set out on his task in good faith, had been overwhelmed by the evidence in favor of the event he was supposed to disprove, and had not only been converted but had written his manuscript to prove rather than disprove the event. Copies of their subsequent book can still be found in libraries.

THE ASCENDED LORD

Isaiah 53:11

Only very rarely in the Old Testament is the ascension of the Lord Jesus even so much as hinted at. Isaiah, with His usual clear vision, catches a glimpse of it and records it, fittingly, in this great chapter which treats at such length the sufferings and humiliation of Jesus.

1. THE LORD'S REDEEMED PEOPLE
   a. A saving Christ
      ("the travail of his soul")
   b. A satisfied Christ

2. THE LORD'S ROYAL PRIESTHOOD
   a. The greatness of His present work
      ("justify many")
   b. The ground of His present work
      ("for he shall bear their iniquities")

NOTE: It must always be remembered when handling an Old Testament prophecy in this way that we are seeing it in the light of New Testament revelation. The Old Testament believers knew nothing at all about the church or the present age of grace. In only the haziest and sketchiest of ways could they see much of what we can see so fully and so clearly now.

It will surely always be a matter of great astonishment that there is a Man, in a human body, a body wearing still the scars of Calvary, sitting at the right hand of God in glory.

CHRIST'S SECOND ADVENT

Isaiah 53:12

Many of the Old Testament prophets saw Christ's two advents. They saw Him coming to *redeem* and they saw Him coming to *reign*. What they did not see was the long church age in between. They saw two mountain peaks rising one behind the other. They were in no position to see the valley separating the one from the other. Hence in Old Testament prophecy the two comings of Christ are frequently telescoped together. Prophet and hearer alike were unable to unravel the seemingly conflicting truths foretold. Isaiah was no exception. Keen as was his prophetic sight he nevertheless passed unconsciously from the first coming of Christ to the second. It was this feature of Old Testament prophecy which caused some of the rabbis to postulate the theory of *two* messiahs— one to be a sufferer, the other to be a sovereign.

1. THE REALITY OF CHRIST'S AUTHORITY
   based on conquest
   a. Dividing the world with his friends
      ("Therefore will I divide him a portion with the great." The LXX can be translated "I will give him the mighty for a portion.")
   b. Destroying the works of His foes
      ("divide the spoil with the strong")

2. THE REASONS FOR HIS AUTHORITY
   based on Calvary
   a. The dreadful intensity of His sufferings
      ("poured out his soul")
   b. The divine intention in His sufferings
      (1) The indignity He bore
          ("numbered with the transgressors")
      (2) The iniquity He bore
          ("bare the sin of many")
   c. The daily intercession of His sufferings
      ("made intercess on for the transgressors")

HO, EVERY ONE THAT THIRSTETH

ISAIAH 55:1-5

Isaiah's name, significantly enough, means "Salvation of Jehovah." He is known as "the evangelical prophet" because so many of his prophecies ring out the gospel message. Again and again in this very chapter he focusses on the good news of God's full and free salvation.

1. SOMETHING SATISFYING
   a. An astonishing opening (55:1a)
      "Ho!"
   b. An astronomical offer (55:1b)
   c. An astute observation

2. SOMETHING SURE (55:3-4)
   a. First listen (55:3a)
   b. Then live (55:3b)
   c. Then learn (55:3c)
   d. Then look (55:4)

3. SOMETHING SPECTACULAR (55:5)
   a. A spectacular ministry (55:5a)
   b. A spectacular mystery (55:5b)

NOTE: "Without money and without price!" Such is the gospel. Some years ago a speaker at the Moody Bible Institute Founder's Week Conference gave a delightful illustration of this. He had come from the other side of Lake Michigan where, just the day before, they had had a heavy snowfall. As he was shoveling off his driveway and sidewalk, along came two big boys with shovels who offered to help for fifty cents an hour. He hired them on the spot. Behind them came a little fellow, all bundled up, carrying a wooden toy spade. He offered to help too. "Mister," he said, "I work for free!" God works for free. His salvation is without money and without price.

SEEK YE THE LORD

Isaiah 55:6-9

Between God and man there looms the immensity that separates the finite from the Infinite, the creature from the Creator. God has bridged that immeasurable gap in the person of His Son. Isaiah sees that and hence he urges upon us the imperative need for closing in with God's offer of salvation while it is still in force.

1. Something Sensational (55:6-7)
   a. A word of comfort (55:6)
   b. A word of caution (55:7a)
   c. A word of compassion (55:7b)

2. Something Sublime (55:8-9)
   The Lord's thoughts and ways are:
   a. Distinctly different from ours (55:8)
   b. Dimensionally different from ours (55:9)

Illustration: There was a blind man who lived in Jericho, a professional beggar who sat by the wayside—a common-enough sight in Eastern lands. One day he heard the noise of a passing crowd and learned from a bystander that "Jesus of Nazareth passeth by" (Luke 18:37). It was the opportunity of a lifetime. He had heard of Jesus, how He raised the dead, healed the lame, gave sight to the blind. He cried out for help, and his only response to his irritated neighbors who told him to be quiet was to cry the louder. Wise man! Jesus of Nazareth never came that way again. He was on His way to Jerusalem and from Jerusalem He went to Calvary.

THE INVINCIBLE WORD OF GOD

Isaiah 55:10-13

God's words are not like ours. Our words at best are only legislative. We can command but can have no guarantee that our commands will be obeyed. God's words are not only legislative, they are also executive. That is, when God speaks it is done. Just like that! He says, in Genesis 1, "Light be!" Instantly light was. God's Word, today, is housed in the Bible. It has lost none of its power for all that.

1. THE GRACIOUS PROVISION (55:10-11)
   a. The divine source of God's Word
   b. The dynamic force of God's Word
   c. The directed course of God's Word

2. THE GREAT POTENTIAL (55:12-13)
   God's Word brings:
   a. A new-born happiness
   b. A new-born holiness
   c. A new-born hopefulness

ILLUSTRATION: When John Gibson Paton wanted to go to the New Hebrides with the gospel, the British government refused to grant him permission. The islanders were the most dangerous and avid cannibals known. Paton persisted, besieging the lords of the Admiralty with importunate demands. Finally one of the sea lords urged that Paton be allowed to go. "If they eat him," he said, "it will give us an excuse to blow the islands out of the sea." Paton retorted that he had some gunpowder of his own he wanted to try first. He was referring to the Word of God. Later, when a British Royal Commission visited the islands after Paton had evangelized them, it reported that the natives of the New Hebrides were amongst the happiest and most enlightened peoples under the British flag.

JEREMIAH'S FOREVIEW OF THE CROSS

LAMENTATIONS 1:12

Jeremiah was a great sufferer. His agony over the impending doom of his beloved Jerusalem embraced not only the coming Babylonian invasion, with all its attendant horrors, but also the anticipated agonies of Christ on the cross.

1. THE UNFEELING ANTIPATHY OF JERUSALEM
   When Christ was crucified—
   a. The rulers were there.
      They were callous.
   b. The Romans were there.
      They were contemptuous.
   c. The rabble were there.
      They were careless.

2. THE UNEQUALLED AGONY OF JESUS
   "Any sorrow like unto my sorrow"
   Compare His sorrows with those of—
   a. Job
   b. Jonah
   c. Jeremiah

3. THE UNDILUTED ANGER OF JEHOVAH
   "His fierce anger"

NOTE: Jeremiah was forbidden to marry. The sufferings he was to undergo were of such a character that God deemed it best for His servant to remain single. His "lamentations" take up one whole book of the Bible. The first four chapters are each a stylized acrostic, but in the fifth, even though it has twenty-two verses—just as the Hebrew alphabet has twenty-two letters—the acrostic arrangement is swept away by sheer emotion.

VICTORIOUS LIVING

DANIEL 1-3

The first three chapters of Daniel are highly biographical and set before us the basic principles for living for God in an alien and hostile world. Daniel and his three friends, torn away from the comforts and shelter of home and set down in a foreign land, are under tremendous pressure to compromise and conform. They refuse to let the world pour them into its mold.

1. THEIR WALK CHALLENGED (Dan. 1)
   The king's meat

2. THEIR WITNESS CHALLENGED (Dan. 2)
   The king's dream

3. THEIR WORSHIP CHALLENGED (Dan. 3)
   The king's image

NOTE: If Satan can persuade us to give in along any one of these three lines he can neutralize our effectiveness for God.

The first move of the enemy was to change the names of Daniel and his three friends. Their Hebrew names had endings that called to mind the names *Elohim* or *Jehovah*. Their pagan names associated them with heathen deities. It was a deliberate attempt to get them to abandon their faith and adopt, in its place, the religion of the land in which they were held captive. Thus Satan sought to find an ally for himself in the natural forgetfulness of the human heart and in man's ability to get used to almost anything.

THE DEEPER LIFE

EZEKIEL 47:1-10

This great prophecy undoubtedly anticipates the blessings that await the Jewish people in the Millennium. It has to do primarily with the rebuilding of the Temple upon the return of Christ. At the same time, with true instinct, preachers have seized upon this passage as illustrating the deeper spiritual life into which God would lead His own.

1. EXPLORING ITS PATH
   Water to the ankles (47:3)
   The path of the river leads to:
   a. The Sanctuary (47:1)
      The place of devotion to God
   b. The altar (47:1)
      The place of death to self
   c. The wilderness (47:8)
      The place of duty to others

2. EXAMINING ITS POTENTIAL
   Water to the knees: prayer (47:4a)

3. EXPERIENCING ITS POWER
   Water to the loins (47:4b)

4. EXHIBITING ITS PRODUCTIVITY
   a. Victory over dearth (47:7)
   b. Victory over death (47:10)

(Note: It issues into the Dead Sea and cleanses it.)

A RELUCTANT MISSIONARY

JONAH 1-4

In one day Jonah brought a city of a million people to its knees in repentance before God. His story has few, if any, parallels in history. No study of revival can possibly be complete which overlooks Jonah. The revival that broke out in Nineveh set back God's foretold judgment on that city for some two hundred years. Yet all the way through the book we are conscious that God is doing His very perfect work with a very imperfect instrument. He always does!

1. THE WORD FROM GOD (1:1-2)
    a. The multitude (1:2)
    b. The man (1:1)
    c. The message (1:2)

2. THE WORD WITH GOD (1:3—2:10)
    a. The prophet captured by God (1:4)
    b. The prophet cornered by God (1:5-17)
       (1) People used to convict him (1:6-11)
       (2) Providence used to convict him (1:12-17)
    c. The prophet conquered by God (2:1-10)
       (1) His despair (2:1-8)
       (2) His decision (2:9-10)

3. THE WORD FOR GOD (3:1-10)
    a. It was brief (3:1-4)
    b. It was blessed (3:5-10)

4. THE WORD ABOUT GOD (4:1-11)
    a. God is a sympathetic God (4:1-5)
    b. God is a sovereign God (4:6-9)
    c. God is a saving God (4:10-11)

A GENTILE PROPHET

MICAH 6:5-8; NUMBERS 22:1-21; 31:8

Balaam, a Gentile soothsayer from the Euphrates, was hired by
Balak to curse the Hebrew people. Four times he tried to
curse the people, and each time God turned the curse into a
blessing. His four prophetic utterances about Israel are
amongst the most amazing and far-reaching in the Old Testament. Balaam himself was interested in the wages Balak offered him, not in the blessings associated with the Hebrew
people. He taught Balak how to corrupt a people he could not
curse and is set forth in the New Testament as an arch-apostate.

In Balaam we are confronted with—

1. A VERY GREAT PROBLEM
   a. That God should communicate to him
   b. That God should communicate through him

2. SOME VERY GOOD PREACHING
   a. The practical teaching of Balaam
      To Balak: his excellent soteriology
   b. The prophetic teaching
      About Israel: his excellent eschatology
      (1) Israel's separation (Num. 23:9-10)
      (2) Israel's justification (Num. 23:21)
      (3) Israel's sanctification (Num. 24:5-9)
      (4) Israel's exaltation (Num. 24:17, 19)

3 A VERY GRAVE PERIL
  It is possible to confuse gift with grace and light with life.

THE GIANT PYGMY

1 Samuel 10:23

Saul was Israel's first king. He was the people's choice and was hailed with enthusiasm because he stood head and shoulders above any of the people. But Saul turned out to be a poor choice for a king. When he met a real giant, Goliath of Gath, he shook in his shoes.

We are told—

1. How Big Saul Was (1 Sam. 10:23)

2. How Bewildered Saul Was (1 Sam. 9:20)
   He simply could not believe that he was going to be Israel's first king when the news was told him.

3. How Bashful He Was (1 Sam. 10:21-23)
   Humility is admirable, but self-conscious inferiority is not. It is a stumbling block.

4. How Bold He Was (1 Sam. 11)
   Saul's initial moves looked good.

5. How Blind He Was (1 Sam. 13)
   The whole incident was a test to see if Saul would "trust and obey."

6. How Bankrupt He Was (1 Sam. 15)
   For his disobedience Saul lost the kingdom.

7. How Base He Was (1 Sam. 17)
   Imagine Saul, a king and a giant, allowing a teenage lad to go and fight Goliath for him!

8. How Bitter He Was (1 Sam. 18:6-9)
   His resentment and envy of David soon blossomed.

9. How Brutal He Was (1 Sam. 18:11-25, etc.)
   He sought in every way to accomplish David's murder.

10. How Bad He Was (1 Sam. 28)
    He broke one of the strictest commandments of the Law by resorting to witchcraft for guidance. When the door of heaven was closed to him he knocked on the door of hell.

THE NAMES OF GOD

SONG OF SOLOMON 1:3

In the Old Testament God revealed Himself by means of the various names by which He called Himself. Three primary names for God appear in the Old Testament— *Elohim* (El, Elah), *Jehovah,* and *Adonai* (Gen. 1:1; 2:4; 15:2). Together with these primary names are numerous compound names, as when tributary thoughts are brought into conjunction with the main Elohim or Jehovah streams. Consider, for instance, the wonderful compound names for God in His character as Jehovah, the covenant-keeping God.

1. JEHOVAH-JIREH (Gen. 22:14)
   "The Lord who provides"

2. JEHOVAH-SHALOM (Judg. 6:24)
   "The Lord who gives peace"

3. JEHOVAH-ROPHEKA (Exod. 15:26)
   "The Lord who heals"

4. JEHOVAH-TSIDKENU (Jer. 23:6; 33:16)
   "The Lord our righteousness"

5. JEHOVAH-SHAMMAH (Ezek. 48:35)
   "The Lord who is there"

6. JEHOVAH-NISSI (Exod. 17:15)
   "The Lord our banner"

7. JEHOVAH-MEKADDISHKEM (Exod. 31:13)
   "The Lord who sanctifies"

NOTE: All these Jehovah titles are hidden in Psalm 23. It is a most instructive and heartwarming way to expound this psalm —just go through and illustrate each of these names of Jehovah in the words of David.

THIS GENERATION

PROVERBS 30:11-14; MATTHEW 23:33-36; 24:32-34

In His Olivet discourse the Lord Jesus spoke of a generation that would witness end-time events culminating in His final return to earth. The phrase in the Proverbs, "there is a generation," casts much light upon the things that will characterize the generation that will witness the Lord's return. We cannot help but see its likeness to our own generation in the features underlined.

1. A CURSED GENERATION
   The writer of Proverbs 30 prefaces the whole chapter by telling us he is writing "prophecy" (v. 1), as the King James Version translates the Hebrew word. (It can also be translated as "oracle.")

   He foresaw—

   a. A furious generation (30:11)
      A generation that curses father and mother
   b. A filthy generation (30:12)
      A generation of young people who are pure in their own eyes but morally filthy in God's sight
   c. A fearless generation (30:13)
      A generation that knows no fear of any authority, divine or human
   d. A fierce generation (30:14)
      A generation addicted to murder and violence

2. A CRISIS GENERATION
   It is the generation that will strut across the earth just prior to the Lord's return.

NOTE: On July 11, 1977, *Time* magazine published a full-length article about the coming generation of young people. "A new, remorseless, mutant juvenile seems to have been born," it says. The whole article is one long commentary on the above.

THE INCENSE

EXODUS 30:34-38; PSALM 141:12

It was patented in heaven. God forbade anyone to make anything like it. It contained four main ingredients, with a pinch of salt added. It was burned upon the golden altar of incense in the holy place of the tabernacle just before the veil. Its ascending fragrance filled the holy place and filtered through into the holiest of all, where God was enthroned upon the Mercy Seat. The incense clearly typifies prayer.

1. HOW THE INCENSE WAS BLENDED
   a. The stacte
      Patience in prayer
      The etymology of the word suggests "to drop" or "to distil"—like the dew, which settles only in stillness and quietness.
   b. The onycha
      Penitence in prayer
      This fragrance was obtained by crushing a perfumed mollusk found in the sea. It suggests being crushed in the presence of God.
   c. The galbanum
      Praise in prayer
      The etymology of the word points to fat or to the uprising sap of a plant, that is, to its strength and virility.
   d. The frankincense
      Petition in prayer
      The word means "to be white," reminding us that our petitions must be pure. The tree that yields it grows on bare, inhospitable rocks. Nothing this world has will sustain prayer.

2. HOW THE INCENSE WAS BURNED
   It was burned morning and evening on the altar with coals taken from the brazen altar of sacrifice.

THE EDENIC COVENANT

This is the first of eight covenants of Scripture. A covenant is
an agreement, or what we would call today a contract. It is an
agreement into which God enters with man. The terms of one
agreement cannot be carried over to another agreement unless
very good reasons exist for doing so. Usually the covenants
are self-contained and exclusive. This first covenant is con-
cerned with man's life in the Garden of Eden. Man is viewed
in all his pristine glory, fresh from the hand of his Creator,
innocent and perfect.

1. THE PROVISIONS OF THE COVENANT
   a. Man's duties explained
      (1) Parental
          Multiply and fill the earth
      (2) Pastoral
          Adam was to be both a gardener and a guardian in
          the perfect environment in which he was placed.
   b. Man's diet explained
      A strictly vegetarian diet
   c. Man's domain explained
      He was given dominion over the works of God's hand

2. THE PROHIBITION OF THE COVENANT
   Man was to abstain from eating of the tree of knowledge
   of good and evil.

THE ADAMIC COVENANT

GENESIS 3:14-19

The Adamic covenant was given to Adam after the Fall and covers life under the new conditions in a sin-cursed earth.

1. NEW LAWS
   a. Doom pronounced
      (1) The curse
         (a) On the serpent
         (b) On the soil
      (2) The calamity
         (a) The woman: sorrow, subservience
         (b) The man: sorrow, sweat
   b. Death proclaimed
   c. Deliverance prophesied
      (1) The first prophecy of a Saviour
         The seed of the woman
      (2) The first provision of a substitute
         The sinners clothed with skins

2. NEW LIMITATIONS
   Cherubim were placed at the gates of Eden to bar the way to the tree of life.

NOTE: God's kindness is frequently referred to in the psalms as *loving* kindness and His mercy as *tender* mercy. How like God to begin the judgment with the serpent so that Adam and Eve, awaiting their turn, could first hear the gospel of the coming Seed of the woman! That robbed even the sentence of death of much of its sting.

THE NOAHIC COVENANT

GENESIS 9:1-27

This covenant was given after the Flood. It spells out the new terms of life on the planet and man's new relationship to man. Before the Flood man was ruled by his conscience. Now he is ruled by Law. Noah is given the sword of the magistrate to enforce discipline.

1. THE SOLEMN PROMISES OF THE COVENANT
   a. Regarding the severity of God
      (1) The pledge
          Never again to send a universal flood
      (2) The proof
          The rainbow in the sky
   b. Regarding the sovereignty of man
      The beasts will stand in awe of him
   c. Regarding the stability of nature
      The seasons will not fail

2. THE SIMPLE PROVISIONS OF THE COVENANT.
      A new diet for man
      A flesh diet instituted; many think this was an added protection against the demon world
   b. A new discipline for man
      Human government instituted; murder was to be punished by death (a law God has never rescinded)

3. THE SUBSEQUENT PROPHECY OF THE COVENANT
   a. A sweeping statement
      (1) For Shem—to be custodian of the name
      (2) For Japheth—to be conqueror of the nations
   b. A significant silence
      Ham is ignored
   c. A solemn sentence
      Ham's son, Canaan, is cursed; his posterity were the Canaanites, whose vileness called for almost complete extermination eventually

THE ABRAHAMIC COVENANT

GENESIS 12:1-4; 13:14-17; 15:1-18; 17:1-8

This great covenant was made with Abraham, the founder of the Hebrew race. It is sweeping and comprehensive in its terms, which embrace all of time. It was an unconditional covenant, God guaranteeing to fulfill its provisions. The seal, or sign, of covenant relationship was circumcision.

1. THE GRACIOUS PROVISIONS OF THE COVENANT
   a. The secular provisions
      (1) A place
          The land from the Nile to the Euphrates pledged to Abraham
      (2) A posterity
          (a) An individual Seed
              "In Isaac shall thy seed be called" (Gen. 21:12), thus the Arab peoples were excluded from the covenant; ultimately "the Seed" was focussed in Christ.
          (b) An innumerable seed
              Abraham's posterity to be like the stars, the sand, and the dust
   b. The spiritual provisions
      (1) Personal
          Abraham counted righteous
      (2) Positional
          All nations to be blessed through Abraham—a promise focussing specifically on Christ

2. THE GUARANTEED PROTECTION OF THE COVENANT
   a. Prosperity for those who "bless" the Hebrew people
   b. Punishment for those who "curse" the Hebrew people

3. THE GLORIOUS PROMOTION IN THE COVENANT
   Abraham's name to be great

THE MOSAIC COVENANT

EXODUS 20

"The law was added" says Paul. The Law was disciplinary and temporary. It operated within the general terms of the Abrahamic covenant. It was given to Israel and to Israel alone—the Sabbath, circumcision, the ritual law are to be understood in the context of the nation of Israel.

1. THE SCOPE OF THE COVENANT
   a. The basic expression of the Law
      The Ten Commandments
   b. The broad expansion of the Law
      In all, the Law contained 613 precepts. These were an exposition of the original ten.
      (1) Laws dealing with national righteousness
          Moral laws
          These dealt with such things as—
          (a) Personal behavior
          (b) Public behavior
          (c) Political behavior
      (2) Laws dealing with national religion
          (a) The Sanctuary
          (b) The service
          (c) The sacrifices
          (d) The Sabbaths
2. THE SOLEMNITY OF THE COVENANT
   a. Its repeated warnings
      "Beware"
   b. Its righteous "wages"
      An eye for an eye. The death penalty was imposed for numerous offences, including murder, adultery, witchcraft, beastiality, homosexuality, and kidnapping.
3. THE SEAL OF THE COVENANT
   The Sabbath. As a law, the Sabbath was given to Israel, not to anyone else.
4. THE SPIRITUALITY OF THE COVENANT
   Its function was to convict of sin and to point to Christ as Saviour.

THE PALESTINIAN COVENANT

Deuteronomy 28-30

Like the Law, the Palestinian covenant operated within the framework of the Abrahamic covenant. In some ways it is a specialized addition to the Law. It spells out the terms under which God would permit the Israelites to remain in the promised land and warned of the disasters that would follow if ever He exiled them from it.

1. The Terms of Israel's National Existence
   God's Word must be obeyed from the heart. Almost the whole of Deuteronomy urges this.

2. The Times of Israel's National Exile
   Exiled from the land, the Hebrews would know—
   a. Dreadful persecution
   b. Divine preservation
      They would never be either assimilated or exterminated.

3. The Truth of Israel's National Exaltation
   a. National rebirth
      (1) The tribes to be regathered
      (2) The territory to be restored
   b. National repentance
   c. National restoration
      (1) The punishment of Israel's foes
      (2) The perfection of Israel's future

Note: Many of the statements of the later prophets regarding Israel's fate and subsequent blessing drew their force and fire from the provisions of the Palestinian covenant. Of course, some of the concepts developed by the prophets can be found only in embryonic form in this covenant, but they are there nevertheless.

THE DAVIDIC COVENANT

2 SAMUEL 7:8-19

That Israel would one day have a king was implied in some of the provisions of the Mosaic covenant. For instance, the Law decreed that any future king must initiate his reign by copying out for himself a personal copy of the whole Law. The Davidic covenant was given to King David. It pledges God's word that David's throne would be firmly established and filled, eventually, by God's own Son.

1. THE SUBSTANCE OF THE COVENANT
   a. The promised seed
      (1) His will be the office of Messiah
      (2) His will be the order of Melchizedek
          A Priest-King, something wholly contrary to the tenor of the Mosaic law. That David understood this is evident from Psalm 110:4.
   b. The promised sovereignty
      (1) A perpetual seat of royalty—a throne
          As Messiah the coming Seed would have—
          (a) A heavenly throne
          (b) A human throne
              The throne of his father David
      (2) A perpetual sphere of rule—a kingdom "For ever"
          This aspect pointed to Christ.

2. THE STIPULATION OF THE COVENANT
   a. The constant factor
      "I will." God asserted His intention of fulfilling the covenant to the full. This points to Christ.
   b. The conditional factor
      "If." Disobedience by David's successors would be visited with chastisement. However, God would see to it that eventually the Messiah would sit on David's throne.

THE NEW COVENANT

JEREMIAH 31:31; MATTHEW 26:27-28; HEBREWS 8:8

This covenant was made with the house of Israel and guarantees the coming millennial glory of the nation. However, some of the clauses of this covenant embrace the church.

1. THE BENEFACTORS OF THE COVENANT
   God Himself is the great Benefactor. He stands solidly behind the provisions of this remarkable agreement with the nation of Israel. The terms of the contract are—
   a. Pledged by the word of God
      "I will." The pledge is unconditional.
   b. Procured by the work of Christ
      This is the significance of Matthew 26:27-28, where Jesus refers to His shed blood as "My blood of the covenant" (*New American Standard Bible*).

2. THE BENEFITS OF THE COVENANT
   a. Regeneration
      All Israel, in a coming day, will experience regeneration. "A new heart." This anticipates the commencement of the millennial reign of Christ.
   b. Redemption
      The Hebrew people who enter the Millennium will all be cleansed from sin (Rom. 11:26).

3. THE BENEFICIARIES OF THE COVENANT
   a. The stated beneficiaries
      The *eschatological* clauses in the covenant belong *exclusively* to Israel. Failure to discern this will lead to confusion.
   b. The subsequent beneficiaries
      The *soteriological* clauses in the covenant belong *inclusively* to the church. God has brought us in under these clauses and given us our standing in grace there.

SUBJECT INDEX

SCRIPTURE INDEX